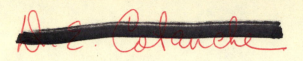

CASE STUDIES IN
EDUCATION AND CULTURE

General Editors

GEORGE *and* LOUISE SPINDLER
Stanford University

CHILDREN IN AMISH SOCIETY
Socialization and Community Education

Old Order Amish Schools in North America, 1970.

CHILDREN IN AMISH SOCIETY

Socialization and Community Education

JOHN A. HOSTETLER
and
GERTRUDE ENDERS HUNTINGTON

HOLT, RINEHART AND WINSTON, INC.
New York · Chicago · San Francisco · Atlanta
Dallas · Montreal · Toronto · London · Sydney

Cover photograph used by permission of Max Tharpe,
photograph on p. 114 by permission of Fred J. Wilson.

Foreword

About the Series

This series of case studies in education and culture is designed to bring to students in professional education and in the social sciences the results of direct observation and participation in the educational process in a variety of cultural settings. Individual studies include some devoted to single classrooms, others focus on single schools, some on large communities and their schools; still others report on indigenous cultural transmission where there are no schools at all in the Western sense. Every attempt is made to move beyond the formalistic treatments of educational process to the interaction between the people engaged in educative events, their thinking and feeling, and the content of the educational process in which they are engaged. Each study is basically descriptive in character but since all of them are about education they are also problem oriented. Interpretive generalizations are produced inductively. Some are stated explicitly by the authors of the studies. Others are generated in the reader's mind as hypotheses about education and its environmental relationships.

The cross-cultural emphasis of the series is particularly significant. Education is a cultural process. Each new member of a society or a group must learn to act appropriately as a member and contribute to its maintenance and, occasionally, to its improvement. Education, in every cultural setting, is an instrument for survival. It is also an instrument for adaptation and change. To understand education we must study it as it is—imbedded in the culture of which it is an integral part and which it serves.

When education is studied this way, the generalizations about the relationship between schools and communities, educational and social systems, education and cultural setting that are current in modern educational discussions become meaningful. This series is, therefore, intended for use in courses in comparative and overseas education, social foundations and the sociology of education, international educational development, culture and personality, social psychology, cultural dynamics and cultural transmission, comparative sociology—wherever the interdependency of education and culture, and education and society, is particularly relevant.

We hope these studies will be useful as resources for comparative analyses, and for stimulating thinking and discussion about education that is not confined by one's own cultural experience. Without this exercise of a comparative, transcultural perspective it seems unlikely that we can acquire a clear view of our own educational experience or view education in other cultural settings without ethnocentric bias.

About the Authors

The authors, both of whom are competent students of Amish culture, have combined their skills to produce this study in socialization. John A. Hostetler, Professor of Anthropology and Sociology at Temple University, was born of Amish parents in Pennsylvania and in late adolescence exceeded the bounds of his culture by obtaining higher education. He holds a Ph.D. degree from the Pennsylvania State University, has done field work in rural communities in the United States and Canada, and as a Fulbright Scholar studied the origins of communitarian societies in Switzerland and Germany. He is author of several books, including *Amish Society*, and is coauthor with Gertrude Enders Huntington of *The Hutterites in North America*.

Gertrude Enders Huntington, an anthropologist, was born at Wooster, Ohio, and now lives in Ann Arbor, Michigan. She attended Oberlin College and was graduated from Swarthmore College. The coauthor studied at graduate schools at Rochester University and Yale University where she received a Ph.D. degree, writing her dissertation on the Old Order Amish community. After teaching school in Wyoming, she taught abroad for two years at the Amerikan Kiz Koleji in Istanbul. Her role in the Amish socialization project, of which John A. Hostetler was project director, was that of resident participant-observer in the community she had observed earlier for her doctoral study.

About the Book

This case study describes a way of life where families are still stable, people live with a high sense of communal obligation, men and women work with their hands, one hears the clop of horses' hoofs rather than the whine of tires, and the school and the community are joined. The Old Order Amish schools are taught by teachers who have no more than an eighth-grade education as far as formal schooling is concerned. In their customary one-room schools they teach "correct knowledge" rather than critical thinking. Schooling among the Old Order Amish is primarily concerned with the development of a Christian character. The properly educated member of the Old Order Amish community values cooperation and humility rather than competition and pride in achievement.

The Amish community and school present a substantial challenge to the basic assumptions and goal orientations of American society and its educational system. In the outside world academic achievement is important. Knowledge for its own sake is significant. Education in the outside society is concerned with a great many things that are unrelated to either an individual's private life or his job. The Old Order Amish see this kind of schooling as detrimental to the relationship between the individual and the community.

It is inevitable, given the divergencies between the Old Order Amish community and its schools and the communities and schools of the outside world, that there should be serious conflict. The struggle to keep the schools under their control is one of the dramatic and often heartrending aspects of contemporary Amish life. The nature of these conflicts is also a commentary on the inability of the majority society, as represented by school officials and state legislatures, to accept deviance.

There is much to be said about the reasons for and the effects of an education in the Old Order Amish schools. The authors, John Hostetler and Gertrude Huntington, have said most of it in a careful but often forceful way. The reader will be able to judge for himself whether and on what terms the Old Order Amish education is effective. As the authors point out in the last chapter, the "how" and "why" of Amish education have many implications for other minorities in conflict with the majority society and its monolithic educational systems.

George and Louise Spindler
General Editors
PHLOX, WISC., 1971

Acknowledgments

A research grant from the United States Office of Education made possible a study of "Educational Achievement and Life Style in a Traditional Society, the Old Order Amish" from June 1, 1966, to August 31, 1969, through Temple University as sponsor. The authors wish to thank Dale B. Harris, Calvin Redekop, Donald A. Erickson, and Marceline Y. Stevens for substantial consultations, and Wayne Miller, James Landing, and Fred Buchanan for their help in the area of schooling. Our special thanks to Amish parents, teachers, and school board members for their assistance.

Contents

CHILDREN IN AMISH SOCIETY
Socialization and Community Education

1 / Amish culture
and educational goals

T HE KITE DANCED and pulled at the end of a long string tied securely to the rail fence that bounded the playground. It looked impressively small, high in the sky. There was a good steady breeze. The teacher and children had used two balls of twine when they "set" the kite during the morning recess. All day it had flown—held in limited freedom by the balanced forces of the wind and the string.

Twenty-six children in eight grades sat in the bright, sunny schoolroom at Meadowbrook. The boys all wore suspenders to hold up their broadfall, dark trousers; the girls wore plain dresses with long aprons. There was no patterned cloth, only solid colors with blues, greens, purples, and browns accented by black shoes. Many of the girls wore black head coverings over neatly braided hair. Four second-graders were at the recitation bench taking turns reading aloud from the *McGuffy Reader* as the other children worked quietly at their desks. The teacher listened to each child read and then, while the third-graders came up to the recitation bench, she answered hands, directing each questioning pupil along the proper path of learning.

Water dripped from the wet snow on the eaves of the new yellow-tiled schoolhouse, each drop making a soft spatter as it hit the fertile ground. Along the muddy lane water trickled in a temporary stream, fed by the melting snow. A frog piped, the birds sounded like spring, and the air and the mud smelled as fresh as the breeze that kept the kite aloft. Rolling fields with an occasional grove of trees stretched towards the horizon. The distant clip-clop of a briskly trotting horse indicated a way of life that needed the small rural school for the education of its children. No pavement, neither road nor sidewalk, could be seen from the schoolyard; the whine of cars and the noise of trucks on the nearest state route did not reach the school house.

Amos sat at his desk copying the lines the teacher had written on the blackboard. By Friday the seventh- and eighth-graders were to have them memorized.

> I live for those who love me,
> Whose hearts are kind and true,
> For heaven that smiles above me
> And waits my spirit, too;
> For human ties that bind me
> For the task my God assigned me

1

> For the bright hopes left behind me,
> And the good that I can do.

He pondered: "I live for those who love me—for heaven—for the task my God assigned me—the good that I can do." He glanced at the clock ticking on the schoolroom wall. Soon the teacher would announce afternoon recess. From his seat he could see that the juncos had not yet flown north, for several were outside the window near the feeding station. He listened to the wind and realized with satisfaction that the kite must still be among the clouds. Today they could not play softball because there was too much mud. Tomorrow he would bring his own kite. In another week the playground would be dry enough for ball. Then the children and the teacher would play vigorous games together.

Meadowbrook School was built only three years ago. The children study a curriculum similar to that of the nearby public school, but in a different context. In spite of a new building and a young teacher, the methods and materials differ little from those of two generations ago. Even though no science is taught and the third grade does not have a unit on weather, all the children are sensitive to the awakening of nature around them.

The days were getting longer and the amount of pressing farm work was increasing. The children were needed at home to learn the practical arts of running a family farm. The teacher was anxious to set her small garden with vegetable plants and flowers and to get ready for the strawberry harvest. Another school year was drawing to an end, a school year still integrated with the agricultural seasons of planting and harvesting, still related to a family unit in which the school-aged children simultaneously are nurtured by the family and contribute physically to the family's security.

Although the Amish school is separated from "the world" outside, it is not separated from Amish life. The school supports the family and the traditions and economy of the Amish community and enables the child to learn both the facts and the roles he needs to function as an Amish person in twentieth-century America. At a time when the cry for relevance is heard from all sides, the Old Order Amish are quietly developing a school system that is integrated with their own life style and therefore relevant.

The Amish have suffered repeatedly from coercive school laws and officials who have not understood their apprehensions about technological progress and the loss of community. Amish parents have served jail terms rather than have their children trained for a way of life not of their choosing. The public school provides suitable preparation for those seeking to participate in mainstream American culture. However, for ethnic and religious groups who think of themselves as "strangers in the land," the expanding role of the public school is threatening. The Old Order Amish are one of several traditional communities who conscientiously reject much of modern technology and new cultural developments. Middle-class values in the public schools threaten a people who want limited isolation from mass communication and protection from the dangers of alienation inherent in the loss of community, a people who strive to cultivate humility and simple living.

AMISH ORIGINS

The Amish are direct descendants of the Swiss Anabaptists of the sixteenth century. The Anabaptists originated in a number of areas simultaneously: there were the Mennonites in Holland and North Germany, the Hutterian Brethren in Moravia, and the Swiss Brethren in Switzerland, all of whom emerged between 1525 and 1536 as forerunners of the "free church" movement (Littell 1964). The period of emergence was turbulent and the dissenters suffered persecution and annihilation for their deviation from the state churches. The attempt to extinguish them was not successful. Those Anabaptist groups who survive share a common heritage: the maintenance of a disciplined community, pacifism, separation from the world, adult rather than infant baptism, emphasis on simple living, and regeneration of character. The Anabaptists were contemporaries of Martin Luther, but went beyond his reforming of the established church. They withdrew completely from the state church and formed voluntary fellowships in imitation of the early primitive Christian church.

The Amish emerged as a dissenting conservative wing of Swiss Anabaptism between 1693 and 1697 (Hostetler 1968:23–44). The name *Amish* comes from their leader Jacob Amman, an elder, who emphasized conservatism. The differences which separated the Amman group from the Swiss Anabaptists (Mennonites) centered on the practice of shunning and the strictness of conformity to specific social and ritualistic practices. The Amman group, for example, began holding communion services twice instead of once each year. Their leader introduced the practice of foot-washing in connection with the communion service and advocated greater uniformity in dress. He taught that it was wrong to trim the beard and that persons who attended the state church should be excommunicated.

The Amish came to Pennsylvania from Switzerland as early as 1727 (Stoltzfus 1954). Today there are no Amish in Europe who have retained the name and principles of the original group. Their descendants in Europe have reunited with the main body of Mennonites or have otherwise lost their Amish identity. It is only in North America that the name and the distinctive practices of the Amish have survived.

The name given to the followers in Europe was *Amish Mennonite* or *Amish*. The name *Old Order Amish* came into common usage in nineteenth-century America to distinguish them from the New or assimilating groups of Amish. Since the Old Order Amish assemble in private homes for worship they are sometimes called *House Amish* to distinguish them from the *Church Amish* who worship in meetinghouses. The persistence of custom and slowness to modernize have been distinctive features of the Old Order. Their communities have remained relatively stable while the dominant culture around them has changed radically.

The Old Order Amish reside principally in the rural areas of Pennsylvania, Ohio, and Indiana, and in smaller settlements in Illinois, Iowa, Wisconsin, Tennessee, Missouri, Maryland, Kansas, and New York. Ontario was settled by a community of Amish in 1824, but several new settlements have been formed there since 1950.

Small communities have recently been founded in South and Central America. The population of the Old Order Amish is presently estimated to be over 60,000 persons.

THE AMISH COMMUNITY AND CULTURAL THEMES

The Community The Old Order Amish are congregational in their church organization. In all settlements their families are divided into ceremonial units called church districts. Each district encompasses a specific geographic area. The size of the church district is limited by the number of people who can meet for the service in a farm dwelling, generally from 30 to 40 married couples and their children. Each congregation has its own ordained officials, usually one bishop, two preachers, and a deacon. The officials are selected by nomination from the members and ordained by lot for life. They receive no formal training before or after ordination and serve without financial support from the congregation. The Amish gather for worship services every second Sunday at a farm home of one of the member couples. On the off-Sunday when there is no worship service, the day is observed as a sacred day, a time for reading the Bible, resting, visiting relatives, and refraining from weekday farm work.

The Amish community has an especially complex organization in those settlements with a number of different types or affiliations of Amish. Such differences arise from liberal-progressive interpretations of the discipline. Since each church district makes its own rules, those districts with similar rules tend to form reciprocal relationships. These relationships are strengthened by exchange visits of preachers, by each supporting the others' disciplinary actions, and by marriage alliances. An Amish group that does not associate ceremonially with another Amish group will say, "Those people are not in fellowship with us." "In fellowship" means there is sufficient agreement in the discipline to permit exchange of visiting preachers. Affiliations have arisen also from church divisions, from long-standing differences in customs, and from differences in leadership by the bishops. But despite these variations, which also have their counterparts in the numerous Protestant denominations, the Old Order Amish generally have the following in common: worship services in the homes of the members, use of horsedrawn carriages, use of the Pennsylvania German dialect, a distinctive plain and simple dress for both men and women, beards but not mustaches for all married men, long hair (which must be parted in the center if parted at all), hooks-and-eyes on dresscoats, and taboos against electricity, telephones, automobiles, and tractors with pneumatic tires. No formal education beyond the elementary grades is a rule of life, and high school or college diplomas are forbidden.

Cultural Themes Five cultural themes in Amish society have significant implications for socialization: separation from the world, voluntary acceptance of high social obligations symbolized by adult baptism, the maintenance of a disciplined church-community, practice of exclusion and shunning of transgressing members, and a life in harmony with the soil and nature. (For more extensive treatment of the culture see the bibliography: Huntington 1956; Hostetler 1968.) Since socialization and therefore also schooling are directly related to the underlying themes of a culture, it is important to understand the basic values of Amish society at the outset.

1. *Separation from the world*: An underlying theme in Amish society is a world view conditioned by Christian dualism, that is, a world containing opposites, such as good and evil, light and darkness. Two biblical passages, perhaps the most often quoted, epitomize for the Amishman the message of separation. The first is: "Be not conformed to this world, but be ye transformed by the renewing of your mind that ye may prove what is that good and acceptable and perfect will of God" (Romans 12:1). It is the duty of a Christian to keep himself "unspotted from the world" and separate from the desires, intent, and goals of the worldly person. To the Amishman this means, among other things, that one should not dress and behave like the world. Another key passage is "Be ye not unequally yoked together with unbelievers; for what fellowship hath righteousness with unrighteousness? and what communion hath light with darkness?" (II Corinthians 6:14). The church, according to biblical teaching, must be "pure," "without blemish," and "without spot or wrinkle." These teachings forbid the Amishman from marrying a non-Amish person or from entering into a business partnership with an outsider. The doctrine applies to all social contacts that would involve intimate connections with persons outside the ceremonial community. The emphasis on separation has given rise to a view of themselves as a "chosen people" or "peculiar people."

The principle of separation conditions the Amishman's contact with the outside world and colors his view of reality and existence. The Amish are forbidden by the precepts and example of Christ to take part in violence and war. When drafted for military service, they apply for conscientious objector status, basing their stand on biblical texts such as "My kingdom is not of this world: if my kingdom were of this world, then would my servants fight" (John 18:36). The Amish find no biblical rationale for self-defense. Like many early Anabaptists they are "defenseless Christians." Problems of hostility are met without retaliation. The Amish farmer, in difficulty with the hostile world around him, is admonished by his bishop to follow the biblical example of Isaac. After the warring Philistines had stopped up all the wells of his father Abraham, Isaac moved to new lands and dug new wells (Genesis 26:15–18). The Amish take this advice literally, so that in the face of hostility, they move to new locations without defending their civil or legal rights. When confronted with school consolidation that makes it impossible to remain separate from the world, they build private schools or migrate to another county, state, or country.

Although the Amish maintain separation from the world, they are not highly ethnocentric in their personal relations with non-Amish persons. They accept as a matter of course other persons as they are, without attempting to judge them or convert them to the Amish way of life. For those who are born and reared in Amish society, however, the sanctions for belonging to the group are deeply rooted in the belief in separation from the world as defined by the church-community.

2. *Voluntary acceptance of high social obligations symbolized by adult baptism*:

The meaning of baptism to the individual and to the community reflects an important core value. In late adolescence, young people are urged by their parents and the ministers to formally join the church by accepting the rite of baptism. Little persuasion is necessary since it is normal for young people to follow the pattern of their peers and be baptized.

Basic to the baptismal vow is the acknowledgement of Christ as the Son of God, belief in the spiritual sovereignty of the true church of God on earth, the "renunciation of the world, the devil, one's own flesh and blood, and confession of Christ as Lord and Savior." The formal confession is not different from other Christian groups. What is significant is the promise to abide by the *Ordnung* and the promise "not to depart from the discipline in life or death."

Great emphasis is placed on walking the "straight and narrow way." Voluntary membership is emphasized, but for one who has been baptized there is no turning back. In support of the religious beliefs an Amish preacher told the court, "We don't go down on our knees for nothing." Applicants are warned not to make a promise they cannot keep. The day prior to baptism the applicants are asked to meet with the ministers, when they are given the opportunity to turn back if they so desire. The young men are asked to promise that they will accept the duties of a minister should the lot ever fall on them. No young person can be married in the Amish church without first being baptized.

3. *The maintenance of a disciplined church-community*: After baptism the individual is morally committed to keeping the rules of the church. For a single person this means keeping his behavior more in line with the rules than before. After marriage the individual assumes a greater responsibility for building the church, which means taking an active part in supporting the community standards. The Amish community is distinct from other church groups in that most of the rules governing life are not specified in writing. These values and norms can be known only by being a participant. The rules for living tend to form a body of sentiments that are essentially a list of "do's and don't's" within the environment of the small Amish community.

All Amish members know the *Ordnung* of their church district. Because most rules are taken for granted, it is usually those questionable or borderline issues that are specified in the *Ordnung*. These rules are reviewed at a special service preceding communion Sunday. They must have been unanimously endorsed by the ministers. At the members' meeting following the regular service they are presented orally, after which members are asked to give assent. A unanimous expression of peace and goodwill toward every member and assent to the *Ordnung* makes possible the observance of communion. Without consensus the communion service cannot be observed.

4. *Excommunication and shunning (Bann und Meidung)* are the church-community's means of dealing with obdurate and erring members and of keeping the church pure. How shunning should be practiced was the central question in the controversy that led the Amish to secede from the Swiss Brethren. The doctrine was intrinsic in the Anabaptist movement from its very beginning. The Anabaptist concept of the church was of a pure church consisting of believers only; persons

who violate the discipline must first be excommunicated, then shunned. This method of dealing with offenders, the Amish say, is taught by Christ (Matthew 18:15–17), and explained by the Apostle Paul (I Corinthians 5:11) that members must not keep company with unrepentant members nor eat with them. The passage is interpreted to mean that a person who has broken his vow with God and who will not mend his ways must be expelled from the fellowship just as the human body casts off an infectious growth. The practice of shunning among the Swiss Mennonites was to exclude the offender from communion. A more emphatic practice was advanced by Jacob Amman. His interpretation required shunning excommunicated persons not only at communion but also in social and economic life. Shunning means that members may receive no favors from an excommunicated person, that they may not buy from or sell to an excommunicated person, and that no member shall eat at the same table with an excommunicated person. If the person under the ban is a husband or wife, the couple is to suspend their marital relations until the erring member is restored to the church fellowship.

The Amish do not emphasize the evangelism of outsiders. They are not as concerned about the redemption of the outside society as they are about the preservation of their own. They will accept outsiders provided they conform to Amish beliefs and practices. Their primary concern is to keep their own members from slipping into the outer world or into other religious groups. Members who wish to have automobiles, radios, or the usual comforts of modern living face the threat of being excommunicated and shunned. Thus the ban is used as an instrument of discipline not only for the drunkard or the adulterer, but for the person who transgresses the discipline of the church. Parents, for example, who send their children to a school beyond that required for living in the Amish community are liable for censure. The same applies to any member who obtains a worldly education.

5. *A life in harmony with the soil and nature*: Implicit in Amish culture is the view that nature is a garden, that man was made to be a caretaker (not an exploiter) in the garden, and that manual labor is good. The physical world is viewed as good and not in itself corrupting or evil. The beauty in the universe is perceived in the orderliness of the seasons, the grandeur of the heavens, the intricate world of growing plants, the diversity of animals, and the forces of living and dying. Amish mores require members to make their livelihood from farming or such closely associated activity as carpentry, mason work, or operating a sawmill. Working in small factories is a trend not approved by the more orthodox Amish. In Europe the Amish lived in rural areas, always in close association with the soil, so that the community was entirely agrarian in character. In America the Amish have found it necessary to make occupational regulations to safeguard their community from the influence of industrialization and impersonal alienation.

The preference for rural living is reflected in attitudes and informal relations for group life, rather than in an explicit dogma. The Amish believe that God is pleased when man works in harmony with nature, the soil, and the weather, and cares for plants and animals. Hard work, thrift, and mutual aid are virtues upheld in the Bible. The city, by contrast, is viewed by the Amish as the center of leisure, non-

Typical farm dwelling in Ohio (A Fred Wilson Photo).

productive spending, and often wickedness. The Christian life, they contend, is best maintained away from the cities. God created Adam and Eve to "replenish the earth, and subdue it; and have dominion over the fish of the sea, and over the fowl of the air, and over every living thing that moveth upon the earth" (Genesis 1:28). Man's highest place in the universe is to care for the things of creation. One Amishman said, "The Lord told Adam to replenish the earth and to rule over the animals and the land—you can't do that in cities." Another said, "Shows, dances, parties, and other temptations ruin even the good people who now live in the cities. Families are small in cities; in the city you never know where your wife is, and city women can't cook. People go hungry in the cities but you will never starve if you work hard in the country."

Lancaster County, Pennsylvania, which is a center of Amish life, has long been distinguished as the garden spot of the nation, representing an intensive method of farming on relatively small holdings. The older residents in Amish communities have accumulated a large amount of agricultural experience and lore reaching back to early colonial days. As farms are handed down from father to son, so are the experiences and the wisdom associated with the care of livestock and farming. The farm economy incorporates the elements of hard work, cooperative family labor, crop and livestock productivity, and saving.

These five cultural themes play an important part in the education of the young. The Amish are not a part of the mainstream of American cultural or religious groupings. Their isolated, intransigent, and withdrawn character has led social scientists to classify them as a sect rather than a denomination. Their negative relation to the larger society enables them to provide for their members a sanctuary from competing value systems. In the face of modern mobility, restlessness, rootlessness, and anxiety, the Amish protect their members against value systems of middle-class society. Worldly success and worldly standards are a threat to the sectarian society, for as sociologists (Niebuhr 1929 and others) have pointed out, many groups which began as sects (such as Baptists, Methodists, and Congregationalists) have, with the acquisition of wealth, become established denominations. Separation is therefore of utmost importance to the Amish way of life.

If we are to understand the goals of Amish education we must fully appreciate the central concept of separation and its manifestations. In order to survive in an industrialized nation like the United States most sects have had to retreat to a spatial and psychic togetherness. As geographic isolation becomes less possible with every new invention, interpersonal relations and cohesion within the community become more and more essential for the successful functioning of the community.

THE GOALS OF EDUCATION: "HUMILITY AND SIMPLE LIVING"

Growing up in a separated society is different from growing up in a mainstream denomination in the United States. In a denomination much of the larger society is affirmed and public education may differ little from the culture of established religions. However, if the Amish child is removed from his community and put into the consolidated school in the larger society, there is sharp discontinuity for him. In the Amish school such arbitrary distinctions between school and life do not exist, for the primary function of the Amish school is not education in the narrow sense of instruction but the creation of a learning environment continuous with Amish culture. By identifying with teachers who identify with them, children acquire understanding essential to becoming an adult. The Amish school atmosphere supports the values and attitudes of the separated community, and the individual is socialized to develop his skills and personality within the small community. Emphasis is on interaction and continuity of lives: of teachers with pupils and of parents with children.

True education, according to the Amish, is "the cultivation of humility, simple living, and resignation to the will of God." For generations the group has centered its instruction in reading, writing, arithmetic, and the moral teachings of the Bible. They stress training for life participation (here and for eternity) and warn of the perils of "pagan" philosophy and the intellectual enterprises of "fallen man," as did their forefathers. Historically, the Anabaptist avoided all training associated with self-exaltation, pride of position, enjoyment of power, and the arts of war and violence. Memorization, recitation, and personal relationships between teacher and pupil were part of a system of education that was supremely social and communal.

The following postulates, derived from an extensive examination of historical sources and verified from observations, express the Amish view not only of formal education, but of human nature and the ultimate goals of training the young.

1. Although children are believed to have an inherited sinful nature through no fault of their own, they are loving and teachable and with the proper environment are capable of assuming responsibility to God and man for their actions by the time they become adults.

2. Parents are responsible for training their children and morally accountable to God for teaching them right from wrong and transmitting to them a knowledge of eternal life.

3. Children are urged not to be idle but to learn to read and write so that they may acquire a knowledge of the scriptures. Learning manual skills that are useful for making a living is also encouraged.

4. Obedience to parents and ultimately to God is a cardinal virtue. Children are not to be self-willed, but well-mannered, quiet, and humble in the presence of others.

5. The family and to a lesser extent the school are believed to have the primary responsibility for training the child for life. Limited individualism within the bounds of faithful adult behavior is the model for the child. It is believed that the child must have an explicit relationship to his parents, siblings, church, community, and school to achieve adequate training for adult life.

6. The school is viewed as an instrument for teaching children the literacy and skills needed to live as productive adults in an environment where values taught in the home are continuous and function throughout the life cycle. The home and the church, rather than the school, are responsible for the religious training of the young.

7. Children during their age of innocence are regarded as pure and not in need of ceremonial baptism. Should they die in their innocence, original sin is not imputed to them on account of the death of Christ. Their entrance into adulthood and the church-community is attained through familiarity with the scriptures, followed by faith and baptism after attaining adulthood.

8. Acceptance of mature social responsibility involves total commitment to the believing church-community and material and spiritual separation from worldly standards, including association and marriage only with members of the believing community and a personal willingness to suffer persecution or death in order to maintain the faith.

Complete separation is not a goal nor do the Amish think of themselves as better than other people. Wholeness and separation are not considered antithetical, but complementary for the continued existence of a prized way of life. Like parents in any society, the Amish want their children to absorb the basic values of their way of life. Many Amish fear the loss of their cohesive spiritual tradition. Their concern is not simply that their children may become "English," but that they may be lost for eternity. Inability to teach their children the Amish way of life affects the parents' relation to God, the community, and themselves. Parents are accountable to God for rearing their children in the faith and to fail to do this is to leave a blemish on the church. To lose one's children to the world is to lose hope of spending eternity with them in heaven.

METHODS OF THE STUDY

This study is not directly concerned with legal or political questions. It focuses on the indigenous processes of nurture and socialization, as well as on formal schooling in the context of Amish culture. It will attempt to illustrate the cultural context of learning—the cultural goals, the institutions, the practices, individual participation in the culture, and pupil achievement—in relation to the whole of Amish society. Implicit in our approach is the assumption that every culture provides guidelines for the rearing of the young and that these guidelines can be articulated by the anthropologist, whether the society be literate or non-literate. Where conflict exists between the public school system and Amish schooling, an attempt will be made to bring anthropological insights to bear on the problem.

Our study deals with the Old Order Amish as distinguished from several more assimilated groups of Amish—the Amish-Mennonites, Beachy Amish, or Church Amish—who have altered their life style by owning automobiles and using electricity and telephones in their homes and who show greater readiness to verbalize personal religious experience in conversation. The whole of Old Order Amish culture is illustrated in this study insofar as it relates to socialization. For more extensive treatment of Amish ethnography the reader should consult the bibliography.

The data for this case study were systematically gathered over a period of four years. The technical aspects of the research appear in *Educational Achievement and Life Styles in a Traditional Society, the Old Order Amish* (Hostetler 1969). The field studies included Amish communities in Pennsylvania, Ohio, Indiana, and several other states with smaller settlements. Socialization practices from infancy through old age were observed while residing in a farm home in a church district. As participant observers, the fieldworkers were identified with a specific family, its network of kinship and visiting patterns, ceremonial functions, and the daily routine of farm and community activities. Interviews were informal and unstructured, but data were systematically obtained and recorded. Repeat visits to the community and shorter visits to other communities with Amish members were important means of obtaining longitudinal data on human growth and community changes. Observations and testing were conducted in Amish schools, in public schools with Amish enrollments, and in a control group consisting of a modern rural school.

2 / Socialization patterns
and the life cycle

IN ALL SOCIETIES occupations are ascribed on the basis of age and sex. Knowledge, values, and attitudes are differentially attributed to each age classification. An individual must recognize the age category to which another person belongs in order to respond properly to him and to expect an appropriate response. Age stages differ from one society to another, but at least seven age-sex categories, according to Linton (1945:66), are universally recognized; Erikson (1950) lists eight. The Amish recognize six age categories, with several less well-defined subcategories, within their culture. The stages in the Amish life cycle are not as sharply delineated as in many cultures, and although each stage tends to correspond to a biological phase, the social functions of each group are culturally determined. Some knowledge of the age structure of Amish society is essential to understanding Amish socialization patterns and the Amishman's participation in his culture.

THE AGE STAGES

In Amish society a person passes through a series of six distinct age categories or stages of socialization as he progresses through life. Different behavior is demanded of him at each stage. The stages, from birth to death, are as follows:

Infancy The first stage covers the period from birth until the child walks. Children of this age are generally referred to as "babies."

Preschool children The second stage covers the period between walking and entrance into school, generally at the age of six or seven. Children of this stage are referred to as little children. Sometimes they are spoken of as children at home, although that phrase more often refers to all children who are unmarried and still eat and sleep under the parental roof.

School children Children attending school are referred to as scholars by the Amish. These children are fulfilling the eight years of elementary schooling required by the state. They attend either public schools or Amish schools and are between the ages of 6 and 16.

Young people Young people or youth are those who have completed eight years of schooling and can therefore do a full day's work. Young people participate

Amish women (A Fred Wilson Photo).

Adults attending a farm sale (A Fred Wilson Photo).

in the social life of their peers as distinct from the family-centered social activity that characterizes the other age stages in Amish culture. Young people are between the ages of 14 or 16 and marriage, which usually takes place in the early twenties. There are several subdivisions within this age stage: Those young people who have finished elementary school but are not yet 16 are generally not full participants in the social life of this group. Those young people who have been baptized are, in many communities, no longer full participants in this age group for they have voluntarily chosen to abide by the rules of the church and are no longer testing the boundaries of their culture. The draft, which removes Amish young men from the community for two years of alternative service, has not become integrated into the age patterning of Amish culture. It can affect either young people or adults.

Adulthood Baptism signifies religious adulthood, but marriage and the birth of the first child brings social adulthood. Generally the time interval between baptism and marriage is relatively short. The major activity during adulthood is child rearing.

Old folks Adults generally retire sometime after their youngest child has married and started to raise a family. They move from the big house into the grandfather house or to the edge of a village. They are cared for by their children and exert a conservative influence as they fulfill their accepted role of admonishing the young.

ADULTHOOD

Age grading in Amish society must begin with a discussion of adults, for the family is the basic unit of Amish culture. The most important family activity is childrearing. Household size may vary from those married pairs who have no children to those having 14 children or more. Studies of family size show that for completed families the average number of children is slightly over seven. Ask an Amishman how big his church district is and he will answer you with the number of families, not with the number of individuals. An Amish schoolteacher will tell you how many families attend the school, and when she introduces the children, she will often introduce them by family rather than by grade.

The Amish family is marked by its stability. Theologically the Amish believe that the commitment to one's spouse is second only to the commitment to God. Husband and wife become one flesh, a single unit separable only by God. For the Amishman, the question of sacrificing his family for his profession never comes up. The family comes first. A job is of no intrinsic importance; it is necessary because it supplies the economic basis for the family. The work of the household should provide vocational education for the children and fulfill the biblical standard, "In the sweat of thy face shalt thou eat bread." Although the Amish family is patriarchal and the husband is the head of the wife, the wife has an immortal soul and is therefore not merely an extension of her husband, nor wholly subservient to him. Her relative position is illustrated by her position in church, where she has an equal vote but not an equal voice.

Parents are expected to serve as examples for the child. An Amish minister admonishes, "Our lives should, by all means, be separated from the world, and be so consecrated, that our children can see by our words and deeds. . . ." Parents do not have individual rights; they have responsibilities and obligations for the correct nurture of their children. An Amishman says, "I am a father. . . . I must teach, train, admonish, chasten, love, and guide my children, and all this with patience and wisdom." In his final admonition before his death, an Amish preacher wrote to his sons, "The responsibility to teach your children lies fully upon you [parents]." Parents are believed to be accountable to God for their children's spiritual welfare. The Amish quote Menno Simons, the sixteenth-century founder of the Mennonites, who says, "Watch over their [your children's] souls as long as they are under your care, lest you lose also your own salvation on their account."

Amish parents act as a single unit when dealing with their children and reinforce one another. Referring to repeated misbehavior of one of her children, an Amish woman said, "We finally decided we would have to spank him if he did it again. He was late again so Amos took him into the bedroom to spank him. I went too because I should help by being there. The boy must know that both of us are concerned." Admonitions to parents in the sermons and in Amish writings are directed not to fathers as such or to mothers alone, but to parents. Parents are taught that if there is a difference of opinion between them, they should discuss it privately and prayerfully and always be of one mind when disciplining the child. The wife is expected to support her husband in all things, especially in his relationship with other people, whether it be their children, parents, or friends and neighbors. The husband in turn should be considerate of his wife on a physical, emotional, and spiritual level. The ideal is to be individuals to one another, but of one mind to all others.

Amish parents are remarkably consistent in the demands they make on their children and in the behavior they expect of them. They constantly reinforce one another and there is general consensus within the community as to how children ought to be raised and how they ought to behave at different stages.

Children function as socializing agents for their parents in a variety of ways. As parents strive to be good examples for their children, they modify their own behavior. In their efforts to teach their children to become good Amishmen, they become better Amishmen themselves. The birth of a child enhances the status of his parents in the community; they attain full adulthood with parenthood. Children take up so much time and energy that the parents are not likely to have time for other interests. Today, because most doctors refuse to come to the house, the large majority of Amish babies are born in the hospital. Medically this is advantageous, but culturally it is not. Home births have a positive value in uniting the family. They demonstrate the wife's unique, dramatic contribution and strengthen her position in the patriarchal family. The husband and wife grow closer by sharing the experience of childbirth. Amish women do not see childbirth as threatening, but as status-enhancing. The most traditional Amish have continued to oppose hospital deliveries and with the help of sympathetic doctors or midwives some of

them still quietly give birth at home. Birth control is not practiced among the conservative Amish.

INFANCY

Babyhood is the stage between birth and walking. The Amish believe a baby is a pleasure. He may be enjoyed without fear of self-pride, for the baby is a gift from God and not primarily an extension of the parents. At this tender age a baby can do no wrong. If he cries he is in need of comfort, not discipline. It is believed that a baby can be spoiled by wrong handling, especially by nervous, tense handling, but the resultant irritability is the fault of the environment, not the baby; he remains blameless. An Amish baby is born into the community. He is never spoken of as "a little stranger," but is welcomed as a "new woodchopper" or a "little dishwasher." Future sex roles are recognized, but there is little difference in the care given a boy or girl. Each baby is greeted happily as a contribution to the security of the family and the church.

Amish babies are rarely alone. They sleep in their parents' room, are moved around the house during the day, and in a large family are held during most of their waking hours. They are diapered and bathed on their mother's lap, not on a hard, cold table or tub; it is a time of happy sociability. Babies are rarely fed on a strict time schedule, but in relation to their own pattern of hunger and the work pattern of the family. Solid food is given at the family table during family meals. The family attitude is one of sharing its good food with the baby. Babies as young as five or six months don't eat well if fed alone, they believe. It is generally thought that everyone eats better in a group; eating is an important social activity. When parents are visiting, at church, traveling, or ill, friends and members of the extended family help with one another's babies. During the first year of life the baby receives solicitous care from a large number of Amish of all ages.

The relaxed handling of Amish babies within the home or the community is quite different from the care taken of them when mother and baby make an excursion into the world. The baby is tightly wrapped and covered, often hidden in his mother's shawl. Even his face may be covered in order to protect him from the "bad air." Passing strangers would probably not realize that the mother was carrying a baby. The traditional Amish dislike having their babies cared for by outsiders or even noticed by them. The way the baby is handled when the mother is shopping or traveling shows the Amish distrust of the outside world and the parents' efforts to protect the baby from its malevolent influence. Old Order Amish parents give generous attention to their babies' needs, both physical and social. This care equips the baby to trust himself and those around him (Erikson 1950:247). Babies are enjoyed by the Amish; they are believed to be gentle, responsive, and secure within the home and the Amish community, but vulnerable when out in the world. Babies are not scolded or punished, and there is no such thing as a bad baby, although there may be a difficult baby.

LITTLE CHILDREN

The preschool stage lasts from walking until entrance into elementary school. During his preschool years the Amish child is taught to respect and obey those in authority, to care for those younger and less able than he, to share with others and to help others, to do what he is taught is right and to avoid that which is wrong, to enjoy work and to fulfill his work responsibilities pleasantly. The parents' task in these years is to create a safe environment for their children. The parents live separated from the world, maintaining the boundary for their children and striving always to protect them from both physical and moral danger.

The children are taught to respect authority, and respect is shown by obedience. The Amish do not strive for blind obedience, but for obedience based on love and on the belief that those in authority have deep concern for one's welfare and know what is best. Children learn this relationship between authority and responsibility very early. The four-year-old child is expected to hand over his toy to the three-year-old if the three-year-old cries for it, but in the parents' absence the three-year-old should do what the four-year-old tells him to. However, the older child may not make arbitrary demands of the younger, and he is expected to cajole rather than force him into cooperation. The children learn in this way that authority is closely linked to responsibility for others. Those in authority must be obeyed, but they do not simply give orders; they also nurture and protect those under their authority.

Most traditional Amish parents teach obedience by being firm and consistent, rather than by violent confrontations or single instances of breaking the child's will. The switch is used freely, but not harshly. In their handling of disobedience, the Amish vary considerably as to the age at which and degree to which they require obedience, in the lengths to which parents will go to get obedience, and in the emotional attitude of the parents in handling a disobedient preschooler. None of the Amish condone willfulness, stubbornness, or defiance on the part of the child, but they may have different opinions as to whether a child's behavior is caused by stubbornness or lack of understanding. The traditional Amish are matter-of-fact rather than moralistic in dealing with their children.

Work is perceived as helping others and fulfilling one's responsibility to them. A child is rarely thanked for doing his chores. Thanks are not expected for carrying out responsibilities. More often the parent may make a simple statement, "Now the floor is clean." The child is rewarded by the task having been accomplished. Work well done is its own reward. Children are trained to help one another rather than to be independent. Thus a four-year-old child will get the boots for the two-year-old and put them on for him, then instead of putting on his own boots he will wait for his older sister to help him. Although the Amish girls always wear dresses and the little boys, after they are toilet-trained, wear trousers, there is little difference in tasks they are taught to perform. Boys are encouraged to like horses and machinery, but children of both sexes accompany their father around the farm and help their mother with simple household tasks.

Young preschool children may scream to get attention or to solicit adult protection from teasing by another child or from the aggression of an age-mate. This is not acceptable for an older child, who is expected to be able to cope with the situation without summoning adult help. Tears are permitted anyone in response to deep emotion, but are discouraged as a response to physical pain or self-pity.

Amish preschool children have great freedom of movement as they accompany their father around the farm, care for a younger sibling, or run simple errands for their mother or grandmother. They are encouraged to be useful but are not pushed to tasks beyond their ability. The environment is neither harsh nor over-protective. Initiative in the physical realm is encouraged, but intellectual initiative or asking

Young Amish children (A Fred Wilson Photo).

questions is severely channeled. Thus, using Erikson's classification (1950:251) of this stage as autonomy-versus-doubt, there is a dichotomy in the development of the Amish child. The Amish child develops the feeling that his physical participation in the world of adults is good, but that his questions are often a nuisance or silly. He acquires a sense of caution about initiating new ideas. Instead of asking how or why, he learns to observe and imitate on a behavioral level.

The presence of the father in and around the home is considered necessary for the proper upbringing of preschool children. As more Amish fathers work in

Amish father and young child (A Fred Wilson Photo).

specialized jobs such as carpentry that take them away from the home for part of each day, there is some concern expressed that the children cannot be properly taught.

The community as well as the family has an essential role to play in the socialization of the preschool child. Preschool children attend church with their parents; they sit through the long service—the girls usually with their mothers, the boys often with their fathers—learning to be considerate of others, quiet, and patient. After the service they share in the community meal and perhaps take a nap on a big bed with other Amish babies. The rest of the time they play freely and vigorously about the house and yard, safe in the presence of many adults who care for them and guide them. If a small child suddenly feels lost, someone quickly returns him to a member of his family. To the preschooler the community seems to be composed of many people, all of whom know him and protect him. He is comfortable and secure within the encompassing community.

Preschool Amish children are kept as far away from the outside world as is practical. When shopping with their parents, they stay very close to them. Little Amish children are not introduced to non-Amish and are not taught about the world outside the community. They may know the exact location of many farms, but not the road to the nearest city.

The Amish generally do not send their children to kindergarten. A 1937 policy states (Beiler 1961:7): "Kindergarten is not sanctioned by the Amish people. Children of this age should be under parents' care. The nurture and admonition that Moses received while under the care of his mother was implanted so deep, that after being taught the wisdom of the Egyptians, [he] chose rather 'to suffer affliction with the people of God, than to enjoy the pleasure of sin for a season.'" In some communities children who will be first-graders in the Amish school the following autumn will visit school in the spring to become acquainted with the new surroundings.

SCHOLARS

The children in this stage, between the ages of about 6 and 15 years, are called scholars. Throughout the school years the family continues to be the primary locus for the child's socialization. Amish families continue to teach their school-age children the same attitudes and values they taught to their preschoolers, and they maintain much the same relation to them in respect to the community and the world. The parents' role is protective and supportive as well as didactic. The parent has the responsibility to punish transgressions, but also the power to forgive. Punishment is used primarily as necessary for the safety of the child: for his physical safety ("stay away from that nervous horse"), for his cultural safety ("be respectful to older people"), for his legal safety ("don't hunt without a hunting license"), or for his moral safety ("be obedient"). Rewards are used to develop the right attitudes in the child: humility, forgiveness, admission of error, sympathy, responsibility, and appreciation of work. Children are motivated primarily by concern for other people and not by fear of punishment.

Children work as well as play together (Photo by Vincent R. Tortora).

The Amish, even those who have their own schools, emphasize that children are the responsibility of their parents; the school and the church are supplemental. The parents must see that their children stay within the discipline of the church. If they do not, the preacher or deacon should talk to the parents, not to the children, about their laxness. The school's task is to cooperate with the parent to preserve the faith taught by the parents, for it is the role of the family, not of the school or even the church, to make Christians of the children.

The parents of school-age children are not only teaching their children Christianity, they are also teaching them the work skills necessary to live an Amish Christianity. By the time the child is eight or nine he begins to have fairly demanding tasks to perform. Boys tend to help their fathers and girls work with their mothers. But everyone helps, regardless of sex, where he is most needed. Formerly the Amish felt secure enough about their children of six or seven, to hand them over to the world for their schooling. During the last 35 years, however, changes in the public schools and in the surrounding rural American culture have created greater problems for the Amish. Modern consolidated schools are not suitable agents of socialization for the Amish child. Two reactions to the disruptive influence of the public school are possible, both of which are currently being tried. The first is to tolerate the public school, attempting to isolate its influence and to counteract the disruption it causes. The second solution is for the Amish to build and conduct their own schools, a new undertaking for the Amish community.

The primary function of the Amish school is to teach Amish children the three R's in an environment where they do not have to learn the assumptions of twentieth-century America, where they can learn discipline, true values, and getting along with each other in life. Participants in a county Amish school meeting reported that "our goal should be that the church, the home, and the school should teach the same things. Let us not confuse our children, but help them to fill their places in the church and community." By contrast the public schools train children to function as individuals, and to find a community of their choosing in the world.

Amish elementary pupils generally have similar experiences within their families and within the community, but their contact with the world differs greatly, depending on whether they attend a public school or an Amish school. Oversimplifying somewhat for purposes of illustration, we will contrast the two types of schools as socializing agents for the Amish child of school age. A primary difference between the public and the Amish school is its relation to the community. The public school is a part of the world and the Amish feel that they have little hope of affecting it. Amish parents, therefore, participate minimally in the public schools. The Amish build their own schools, not only with their own money, but also with their own hands. They make all the decisions, within the limits of the state law, about the school calendar, the subjects to be taught, the teachers to be hired, and the books to be used. Parents, ministers, and travelers from other Amish communities are always welcome visitors at the school. Physically and emotionally the school belongs within the Amish community.

Operating private schools introduces certain problems within the Amish community. Supporting an Amish school is sometimes an economic strain. A certain amount of borrowing of techniques and practices from worldly schools is necessary. Therefore, unless carefully managed, the boundary between the world and the church may become blurred. This is especially true if the community is not "of one mind." Misunderstandings sometimes arise because the roles of the teacher and the school board members are still in the process of becoming institutionalized. Regional and national meetings, attended by teachers, board members, and ministers, are helping to define the teacher's role within both the school and the larger Amish community. Some Amish parents are also concerned that the children learn too little about the world when they attend only Amish schools. They realize that one must understand the world fairly well in order to reject it selectively and in such a way that survival is possible within the twentieth century. They feel that the children should master English and understand the ways of worldly people to the extent that is necessary for business transactions with them.

Both the public schools and the Amish schools teach the three R's, but their

Children of all ages learn by helping their parents (Photo by Vincent R. Tortora).

methods are quite different and their attitudes toward the ultimate use of the knowledge is very different. The public schools use a greater variety of material and stress speed, sometimes at the expense of accuracy. The Amish schools tend to use a more limited amount of material, but the children learn it thoroughly. They stress accuracy rather than speed, drill rather than variety, proper sequence rather than freedom of choice. The public school tends to teach subject matter as a tool needed by the child to achieve social mobility and to realize his highest individual potential. The Amish schools teach the same material, but they aim to help the child become a part of his community and remain within his community. They emphasize shared knowledge rather than individualized knowledge and the dignity of tradition rather than progress.

In the public school, children are separated from their siblings and placed into narrow age groups. Individual achievement is emphasized. In Amish schools brothers and sisters are in the same room, age grading is not so rigid, and group excellence or group competition is used as a stimulus. A whole school will strive to have a perfect score in spelling; a chart will be kept of each class's average in the arithmetic test scores. This is similar to the use of competition in the Soviet children's collectives, where competition is used to enhance the group and build group responsibility rather than to bring praise to the individual (Bronfenbrenner 1970:50).

Public schools tend to teach that weakness is bad and should be overcome by the individual; Amish schools assume that all individuals are weak and that they need help from one another and from a higher power as well as individual effort in order to improve. Within the public school the child is regarded as a citizen and an intellect; within the Amish school, as a future Amishman and a soul. In the public schools a teacher's academic training, knowledge of his subject, and teaching techniques are the criteria for hiring. In the Amish schools the teacher's example in daily life and wisdom are more important than training and factual knowledge. Amish teachers have no tenure, for obviously someone who turns out to be a poor teacher is not fulfilling the role God intended for him and should do some other, more suitable kind of work. Public elementary school is conceived as preparing the child for high school, not as sufficient in itself. The Amish school assumes that the child will go on learning for the rest of his life, but that his formal schooling will end with the eighth grade.

The greatest dangers of public school for the Amish child are not the differences in attitudes between his parents and his teacher, not the specific subject matter taught in the public school, not such frills as visual aids and physical education, but the possibility that he may form close personal friendships with non-Amish children and that he may become too comfortable in the ways of the world. Continuity with faith, family, and community would then be broken.

During his school years the Amish child spends most of his time outside of school with his family at home or visiting as a member of his family at the homes of friends and relatives. The family attends church as a unit, and people of all ages listen to the same service. The Amish schoolchild, unlike the typical suburban schoolchild, is usually in a mixed age group rather than isolated with his peers (Bronfenbrenner 1970:96–102, 115). If he attends an Amish school his classroom is shared with seven other grades. He knows many adults in addition to his parents, and they have a comfortable interest in him and his development.

During the elementary school years Amish children are encouraged in their efforts to make things with their own hands. Girls cook, bake, sew, and make things for their playhouses. Boys often build toys or birdhouses, and they help with the farm work, learning the necessary routine of feeding poultry and livestock. Their sense of industry is enhanced by the work of their hands, by being praised and rewarded with the results, and by being allowed to finish their products. The child in an Amish school is more than a personality in a schoolroom. His world includes his home and family, which play a central role in his development. Whether the child develops a sense of industry or inferiority (Erikson 1950: 258) during the school years depends to a great extent on all the adults in his life—not only the schoolteacher. He has many role models and informal teachers.

YOUNG PEOPLE

The young people are those in the age category between 14 or 16 years of age and marriage. In this stage the Amish individual progresses toward adulthood in an orderly, clearly defined manner through a series of accepted stages. Two governmental institutions, schooling and the draft, threaten this order by prolonging childhood in one case and adolescence in the other. Forcing an Amish person to attend school daily places him in the child category, for the hours spent in school prevent him from doing a full day's work, which is the criterion for achieving the status of young adult. The alternative service program of the draft removes the young man from the community and from the opportunity to accept an adult role, thereby extending his adolescence. When the individual is prevented by the state from achieving a status position within his culture believed to be his due, both the individual and the culture suffer.

Compulsory schooling appeared with the growth of the industrialized state and is tied to industry, government, and the military. In the United States, school is a prerequisite for membership in a managerial middle class. The Amish reject membership in a managerial middle class; they reject urbanization, industrialization, and participation in the armed services, and they reject the training that would prepare them for unacceptable occupations. They withdraw their children at the end of elementary school—or in some areas at the end of vocational school—to train them within the home and the community to become skilled in and to enjoy the work they will actually be doing as adults.

The Amish have consistently maintained that further formal education beyond elementary school is not only unnecessary but detrimental to the successful performance of Amish adult work roles. Recent studies seem to bear out these assumptions. Ivar Berg (1970:50) suggests that the over-educated are less productive, whether they are factory workers or elementary school teachers, and that in many kinds of work on-the-job training is more important than educational credentials. Certainly the skills the Amish need are best learned by doing. The enjoyment of physical labor can be learned better by laboring than by studying in a classroom.

For an individual to become Amish he must be kept within the Amish community, physically and emotionally, during his crucial adolescent years. High school removes the Amish child from the community by changing his status, by removing him from it physically for many of his waking hours, by teaching him skills and attitudes that are disruptive to his way of life, and by enabling him to form personal friendships with non-Amish young people. The school is disruptive both in what it teaches the Amish child and in what it prevents him from learning. If he is in school, he cannot attend sales and learn how to buy and sell in the worldly market, and he cannot attend work bees or weddings or church services for visiting preachers and learn adult roles of social integration. Amish children who attend high school experience conflict and anguish that often last well into adulthood.

In this age stage excursions will be made out into the world, but, it is hoped, not until late in adolescence. Nor should these excursions last for long. They should never remove the young person to a great physical distance from an Amish community. Amish young people may work for "English people," in this way learning about the world, but they must return home every weekend. Young people may work in small rural factories, but they return home in the evening and do not join labor unions. Even this amount of contact with the world is not permitted until

Adolescent Amish boy (A Fred Wilson Photo).

almost the end of this age stage, and if it appears that the young person is not ready for this degree of contact, his parents may try to make him quit his worldly work.

During adolescence the peer group is of supreme importance, for most of the Amish young person's socialization takes place within this group rather than within the church or the family. If the young person's peer group remains Amish, he has a reference point, a balance, and a support. Even though as an individual or as a member of this Amish peer group he transgresses many rules and crosses most of the boundaries between the Amish community and the world, he will eventually return to the church and become a lifelong Amishman. However, if during this stage he makes English friends and identifies with an alien peer group, even though he is well behaved, he will probably leave the Amish church never to return.

Courting age, called *rum springa* or "running around," begins at about 16. Attendance at Amish young people's gatherings are important aspects of socialization during this period. The most important gathering is the Sunday evening singing attended by the young people. Aside from hymn singing, it is an evening of informal association, where an hour or more is spent visiting and joking, and where dates are arranged. Other social occasions are at weddings, cornhusking bees, and various kinds of mutual aid parties or "frolics." In addition to taking his girl home on Sunday evenings after the singing, in some communities a young man who is going steady will see his girl friend every other Saturday evening at her home. When Saturday evening comes he dresses in his best, and making a quiet departure from his home, he may leave the impression that he is going to town on business. Secrecy pervades the entire period of courtship regardless of its length. Most boys marry between the ages of 22 and 24. Girls tend on the average to be a year or more younger than boys at marriage.

The choice of a mate is conditioned by the values of Amish culture. A boy must obtain a partner from his own Amish faith, but not necessarily from his own community. Young people intermarry among Amish districts of the same affiliation and among settlements that maintain "fellowship" with one another. Marriage must be endogamous with respect to religious affiliation, for an Amish person who marries a non-Amish person is excommunicated and shunned.

First-cousin marriages are taboo and second-cousin marriages are discouraged, but do occur. The newly married couple receives economic assistance from both of their parents, often consisting of furniture, a cook stove, livestock, and basic farming equipment. Every mother is concerned that each of her children receive a home-made quilt and comforter. These are often made several years in advance so they will be ready when marriage takes place.

Conscription is especially disruptive to the Amish. Throughout their history the Amish have been pacifists, refusing to serve in any army. Today drafted Amish young men spend two years performing alternative service under the Selective Service classification of 1-W. A memo from Selective Service instructs local draft boards that suitable 1-W employment should "constitute a disruption" in the life of a conscientious objector (Local Board Memorandum No. 64, September, 1968). This is in addition to the requirements that (1) the work must contribute to the national health, safety, or interest, (2) the work should be performed outside the community in which the person resides, and (3) the job should be one that cannot be readily filled from the competitive job market. The Selective Service program is more disruptive to the Amish community than is apparent from the number of individuals actually in service. Those who are drafted must live outside the Amish community, often alone, in a city, perhaps wearing non-Amish clothing while at work. These measures separate the young men from community control and to a limited extent make them non-Amish.

Baptism has always been an important *rite de passage* among the Amish, for it signifies not only total commitment to the believing church-community, physically and spiritually separated from the world, but also admission to adulthood. If the drafted young man is baptized before his 1-W service he cannot live physically separated from the world, as he is pledged to do. If he is not baptized before his service, he has not committed himself to the church-community, and so is more vulnerable to outside influences. Not only does 1-W service make less clear and less meaningful the rite of baptism, it also affects marriage. Is it best for a young man to marry before, during, or after his service? If he goes into the world without a wife he may form friendships with non-Amish girls, and because marriage must be "in the Lord"—that is, with a co-religionist—such friendships are dangerous. If he has a wife, she helps protect him from worldly influences, but they start their married life with modern conveniences, electricity, and telephones that are hard to give up when they return to an Amish way of life. And what about children who are born outside the community? During 1-W service both the Amish men and their wives learn non-Amish work patterns and may receive training they will never use on an Amish farm. They work exclusively in a non-Amish environment with non-Amish people.

Probably the most disruptive influence for the young men is learning to know kind, highly verbal fundamentalists who are not Amish and who challenge the specific rules of the Amish church. The young men in 1-W service often receive higher wages than they would within the Amish community and sometimes they are tempted to work longer than the required two years. Many young men and even couples find the adjustment back to the watchful community difficult after the autonomy and anonymity of city living.

The most traditional Amish refuse alternative or 1-W service. As one member said, "God did not mean for the Amish to take the way of 1-W service. He is not blessing or prospering us for accepting 1-W service. It is better for the Amish to go to prison, though it is hard. God is with them there." In contrast to the men who accept alternative service, those few who go to prison generally return to the Amish community stronger in their faith and more secure in their conviction. They do not go through a period of uncertainty when they return. The rite of baptism retains its significance and is perhaps enhanced for these Amishmen, for the time they spend outside the community serves to clarify the boundary between the world and the church. It enables them to identify with the martyrs of their heritage and it reinforces their belief in the necessity of separation from an evil world.

A certain degree of adolescent rebellion has become institutionalized among the Amish. The Amish child is raised in a carefully protected environment by relatively authoritarian parents and teachers. However, by the close of this age stage the Amish young person will have made the two greatest commitments of his life: he will have decided to join the church and will have chosen a spouse. He is expected to make these commitments as an individual with the help of God. In order to make such important decisions he must establish a degree of independence from his family and to some extent from his community in order to develop his own identity. This is done in many ways, most of them carefully institutionalized. First, the family relaxes some of its tight control over the young person. He goes to social gatherings of his peers rather than having all of his social life with his family. This is believed to be a time during which the young person learns what it means to be Amish. The community does not officially have control over him. During this period he often tests some of the boundaries of the Amish community, sampling the world by such means as perhaps owning a radio, having his photograph taken, attending a movie, and occasionally wearing clothes that are outside the *Ordnung*. As long as these forays are discreet, they are ignored by the parents and the community, for it is believed the young person should have some idea of the world he is voluntarily rejecting. One of the reasons courtship is secretive is that this is one of the only means of achieving privacy in a closely knit community and within a large family. The young person is protected by a degree of institutionalized blindness on the part of adults who thereby give him some freedom.

Earlier in his life the Amish child accepted being Amish as part of his identity. During this age stage he strives to determine what it means to him to be Amish. His family and the community help him by overseeing his vocational training. Both the young Amishman and young Amish woman work for a variety of different people during these years, learning various acceptable vocational roles and getting, through their jobs, a knowledge of other Amish families and other Amish communities and a glimpse of the world. During their working hours the young people are respectful of community standards. However, during free time with their peers, there is considerable testing of boundaries and striving for self-knowledge. This period is made much more difficult if the young person attends high school, is removed from the community by the draft, develops close friendships with English young people or becomes interested in a fundamentalist religious group. When any of these things happen, there may be a long and difficult period during which the young person strives towards integration. In the more typical cases, where the Amish young person remains emotionally within the community, there is rarely much role confusion, and in Erikson's terms (1950:261) this age stage could be characterized by ego identity. The typical Amish young person is not an impatient idealist nor is he in search of negative identity. The preparation for this phase of his life began in the cradle, where he was cared for in such a way that he developed trust in himself and his environment. In the stages that followed he developed confidence in his physical participation in the world around him, coupled with some insecurity in the area of manipulating ideas. Amish young people find continuity between what they learned as children and what they experience as adolescents. By the end of this age stage the Amish adolescent is able to bring together his new-found abilities—the things he has learned about himself as a person, a family member, a worker, a member of the Amish peer group—and integrate these images of himself into a whole that makes sense. Within his family and community he arrives at a sense of who he is, where he has come from, and where he is going.

OLD FOLKS

Amish socialization patterns provide the individual with resources for meeting the major problems of aging: the inactivity of retirement, economic insecurity, prestige loss, social isolation, loss of health, and death. The Amish accept aging realistically as a natural stage of human life. The care of the aged does not depend on a single institution; it is part of the total way of life.

The age of retirement for either men or women in Amish society is not rigidly defined by the culture and varies widely among household heads. If his children are married and in need of farms, the father may decide to retire as early as 50. Where pressure for farms is not a consideration, the head of the family may in rare cases decide not to retire until the age of 70. Retirement is voluntary and often gradual rather than abrupt. Even after retirement work and activity do not change much, for grandparents usually assist their married children with work in times of specific need. Health is a factor in determining the onset of retirement. Work expectations can be reduced without fear of losing prestige, and men are not forced to choose between full-time jobs and doing nothing at all. Obligations such as attending funerals and visiting the sick and the bereaved increase with age.

Moving into the "grandfather house" is the normal way of retiring. The old folks move into the adjacent farm dwelling and live from their life savings, which are supplemented by a share in the farm and a modest income from carpentry or other part-time work as long as health permits. Separate living arrangements and inde-pendence of travel are important personal liberties respected by the Amish system of retirement. Grandfather continues to have his own horse and buggy. The Amish do not apply for old age and survivors' insurance benefits. The economic aspects of retirement are not major considerations. What is most important is a mode of life that permits continuity between the generations and associations between grandparents and grandchildren.

Prestige tends to increase with age, so old age brings no noticeable evidence of anxiety due to loss of status. Older men and women both have a formal vote in the church business sessions. The association of age with respect in a patriarchal society tends to strengthen the ties with the past. Old fashioned ways are revered and a knowledge of these ways is perpetuated by the older people. Young farmers ask their fathers for advice on a variety of farm management problems. Mothers ask grandmothers for advice on how to rear their children, even though they do not always follow their instructions. Such interaction between the age groups lessens the strain between the generations.

Social life seems to be balanced between privacy and social involvement. Privacy is available for the elderly individual or couple, while participation in the church and community activity continues naturally. In fact, retirement from church offices, such as those of bishop, deacon, or preacher, is not possible since ordination is a lifetime calling. Psychological isolation and loneliness are not major problems. Togetherness is fostered in religious life, kinship and visiting patterns, and agricultural pursuits of a simple style that permit children and parents to work and live in proximity to each other. The psychological aspects of aging are acknowledged and are met by the community and the family. The slow rate of change and strong community ties in Amish society assure older people of ample opportunities for meaningful social participation to the limit of their energy and mental capacities.

The Old Order Amish people do not build separate institutions or homes for the aged. The aged are therefore not physically removed from their children and grandchildren. The firm teaching among the Amish that children should obey their parents places a moral obligation of reciprocity on the young married people to provide for their aging parents.

The manner in which the culture influences the psychosocial adjustment to aging and illness is an important asset. Ailments are accepted realistically and local physicians are patronized at will. Nonscientific medical beliefs have been observed in Amish society, but what is most marked is an overall concern for the sick in the community. Persons who are too ill to attend religious services are talked about at great length. They are normally visited by relatives and friends Sunday afternoon or during the week. Small gifts of food or other specialties are often given to them. The senile and mentally ill are cared for in the household except when such care would be physically dangerous for the patient or his caretakers. The family and community provide the aged with a sense of belonging and a feeling of being needed. Older people are more free to travel and consequently often do more visiting than other adults.

Elderly Amish people are concerned with others beyond their immediate family, as well as with the welfare of the community and the world within their grasp. Interest in the well-being of others generally overshadows self-absorption and preoccupation with personal needs and comforts. There is time for reflection and the enjoyment of many grandchildren as the individual's major efforts are nearing completion. In the final stage of life there is integrity rather than despair (Erikson 1950:268). The elderly Amish person looks back on his life with satisfaction.

Dying takes place in familiar surroundings rather than in a lonely, impersonal, and mechanical environment. Except for accidental or sudden illnesses, most Amish are allowed to die in peace and dignity surrounded by friends and relatives in their own house. When death occurs, few decisions need to be made by the family that are not dictated by custom. Neighbors and nonrelatives relieve the family of all work responsibility. Young men are appointed to take over the farm chores and an experienced couple takes over the responsibility of managing the household until after the funeral. These appointments are considered a great honor. The managing couple will solicit as many helpers as are needed for cleaning, food preparation, and making burial arrangements. The relatives spend their time in quiet meditation and in conversation around the bier where guests come to see their departed friend and to talk to the bereaved family. The Amish observe the wake by sitting all night around the deceased, and young people gather to sing hymns on at least one of the evenings before the funeral. Amish coffins are made by a carpenter or an undertaker who caters to the customs of the Amish. Pallbearers are selected by the family. Their duty is to dig the grave, assist with the physical arrangements at the funeral, open and close the coffin for viewing, arrange for transportation, and close the grave at the cemetery.

Funerals, especially of elderly people, are attended by large numbers of friends and relatives from various states. Five hundred mourners may be present. Following the burial, it is the custom to return to the house of the deceased for a meal; at this meal normal role relationships and responsibilities are restored. The quietness and seriousness which have prevailed for three days is now broken by normal conversation and interaction. Family members are readily integrated into the ongoing concerns of the community where bereavement is healed by godly and ethnic ties. The belief in eternal life beyond death is also a source of comfort to the mourning family. Death shakes the emotional foundations of the individual, but the major burdens are borne by the church-community.

Buggies tied to a row of trees. The occupants are attending a funeral on the farm (A Fred Wilson Photo).

3/The Amish elementary school

THE RISE OF AMISH SCHOOLS

AMISH SCHOOLS originated in response to state consolidation of public schools in this country. The first Amish school was built in 1925. In 1950 there were 16 schools and in 1970 over 300, with an estimated enrollment of 10,000 pupils. The Amish have suffered repeatedly at the hands of school officials who have not understood their concern for education, or the distinction they make between technology and wisdom, between the critical analytical method and the quest for social coherence in their community life.

Of six main arguments in favor of school consolidation (Loomis and Beegle 1950: 590–591), none are acceptable to the Amish:

1. "Equalization of costs between the poorer and wealthier districts." The Amish do not care if their district is financially poor, for simplicity and modesty are considered virtues.

2. "Better teachers." The Amish do not believe that higher education necessarily produces better teachers, nor that higher salaries insure greater competence.

3. "Superior curricula." The Amish consider the curriculum of the larger schools inferior, for it usually stresses science and lauds technology.

4. "Specialization of instruction and grading of pupils by age groups." The Amish are opposed to specialized instruction, preferring that their children learn only the basic skills of reading, writing, and arithmetic. They consider it a disadvantage to group children only with their age-mates rather than letting them associate in a mixed group, where the younger children can learn from the older and the older children can help the younger.

5. "Social advantages to pupils and to the community." This is considered a danger rather than an advantage, because the Amish wish their children to follow in their own footsteps and not to move on to other occupations or higher-status jobs.

6. "Better administration and superior vision." The Amish are suspicious of administration, for they believe that agreements should be informal and based on the word of the parties concerned. There is little need for administration in small face-to-face groups. The Amish also believe the vision of administrative officials

34

to be inferior rather than superior, for it usually is progress-oriented and based on an exclusive belief in the scientific method.

When the population in the United States was primarily rural and the major occupation was farming, the Amish people had no real objections to public schooling. Some mixing with English or non-Amish children is still considered desirable by many Amish parents. In the traditional country school the Amish child received a little contact with other children. In the rural public school the Amish child was treated as a member of a group rather than as a unique personality. The songs learned were largely religious; they were copied into notebooks and sung in unison, as is done in the Amish tradition. The Amish children achieved their basic skills in reading, writing, and arithmetic, and the school was acceptable to the Amish, even though a considerable portion of the program was neither meaningful nor relevant to the Amish way of life. The method of learning (by oral means and by example) was consistent with the Amish culture. So long as the schools were small and near their farm homes, the Amish were able to moderate exposure to alien values. With public school consolidation these conditions have changed.

When in 1965 the Iowa Amish refused to send their children to the consolidated public school, the state and county officials asserted that the Amish objections were economic rather than religious. From the attorney general's office to local board members, public officials held that the Amish wanted to avoid the expense of hiring certified teachers. Neighbors of the Amish told state officials that religious conviction was not involved in the question of certification. They pointed to the fact that the Amish families had for 14 years used certified teachers in their schools. But what was taken by the non-Amish community to be stubbornness, noncooperation, and a parsimonious attitude toward education was for the Amish leaders a central religious principle with a background of over two centuries of experience. The Amish sensed intuitively what scientists know empirically, that when a secular system of education displaces the indigenous method of training, the basis for a traditional way of life is swept away.

The Amish community requires face-to-face contacts in order to remain viable. Its cohesiveness is based upon personal responsibility and shared values. The primary unit remains small and on a human rather than an organizational scale. As long as the public school maintained this human scale, the Amish were satisfied, and many were active participants in the schools. In one instance, an Amish member of a township public school board in 1895 supervised the building of the public school on a corner of his farm. Sixty years later when the township sold the schoolhouse, made obsolete by consolidation, the Amish community bought the building for $3,240 and established its own school. Many Amish served as trustees or board members of public schools in rural communities; today they form their own schools in direct response to the bureaucratization of small schools and the changes that go with the organizational scale.

The Amish struggle to retain the school on a human rather than an organizational scale has centered around four major issues:

1. *The location of the school.* The Amish insist that their children attend schools located close to their homes in an agricultural environment, so that children can help with the farm work and aspire to become farmers, for farming is a basic tenet in the Amish way of life. Consolidation threatens the homogeneous character of the Amish community and exposes the children to alien values. To avoid these perils the Amish founded one- and two-room private schools.

2. *The training and qualifications of the teacher.* In order to teach their way of life, the Amish want to have qualified teachers committed to Amish values. Their method of teaching is largely based on example and learning by doing. Persons qualified by state standards are incapable of teaching the Amish way of life by the example of their lives.

3. *The number of years of schooling.* The Amish want their children educated in the basic skills of reading, writing, and arithmetic in elementary school. All training beyond that, they say, should be conducive to the Amish religion and way of life. Conflict developed over the number of years of schooling when states raised the age requirement from 14 to 16 and in some instances to 18 years.

4. *The content of education.* The Amish basically object to having their children trained for a way of life that is contrary to their religion. "Public or free schools," they say, "are intended only to impart worldly knowledge, to insure earthly success, and to make good citizens for the state." The Amish say it is the duty of the church-community to prepare their children to live spiritually in this life and for eternity.

The Amish were opposed to separating school from life. The alternatives were these: permit the children to attend the large schools (more liberalized groups have done so), request officials to keep the one-room school open, vote down the consolidation option and higher taxes, ignore compulsory attendance laws after the completion of eighth grade, or open private schools of their own. The Old Order Amish, who have no training in either secondary schools or college, responded to the challenge by building and staffing their own schools.

The Amish have two types of schools: the elementary school consisting of the first eight grades and the vocational school. The latter is an on-the-job training program attended by children who have successfully completed the eighth grade but are not yet old enough to obtain a working permit. They meet as a group under the supervision of the vocational school teacher (see Chapter 5). Amish schools are neither parochial nor private in the sense in which these terms are currently used in America. The schools are built and operated by parents and not by a centralized church organization. They resemble more the pattern of the free schools or academies of colonial America than typical parochial schools.

ORGANIZATION AND FINANCES

Amish society is localized, informal, and familistic. The basic unit of organization is the local church district; beyond the district there is no formal religious hierarchy. The various church districts and geographic communities are held together by kinship ties, visiting patterns, and by familiarity of belief and life style. Just as the churches, which are self-governing units, differ slightly from one another on specific rules of discipline, so the schools vary in local organization and administration. The schools have much in common, but since decisions are made locally, details vary from one school to another, from one community to another, and from one affiliation to another. The small size of the school makes management possible with a minimum of bureaucracy.

All Amish elementary schools are administered by a school board. In most Amish communities each school has its own board, but sometimes several schools are administered by a single board. For example, in Wisconsin there are two schools under one board and in Pennsylvania there are six schools under one board. School boards consist of from three to six members, with one of the members serving as president. Various other positions may be filled by board members or by other elected or appointed individuals. The clerk keeps records of the meetings. The superintendent, director, or committeeman attends meetings on a township or county and state level; he is responsible for knowing any changes in civil law that concern Amish education and for implementing these changes in his school. The treasurer collects the money needed for the functioning of the school, pays the teacher's salary, and is responsible for all the bills. Sometimes this position is divided into three: (1) an assessor, (2) a collector, and (3) a treasurer. The attendance or truant officer is responsible for seeing that the children are not illegally absent from school and that attendance records are forwarded to state officials. In many schools the teacher forwards the reports and the attendance officer is rarely called in. Some schools do not have an attendance officer. These different positions with overlapping rules and responsibilities are confusing to the outsider, but the seeming vagueness and the minor variations from school to school and from church to church are cherished by the Amish, who see in the fluidness of the organization a protection of their congregational social organization.

Board members are elected to their position by the patrons of the school, usually by a vote of all the church members of the district or districts in which the school is located. In some localities, however, the school is supported only by church members who are parents rather than by the whole church, in which case the parents elect the board members. When children of several different Old Order church affiliations (noncommuning churches) attend one school, the members of each different church affiliation may elect one board member.

In Pennsylvania, school board members often serve for a long time. One person has served on the board since the first elementary school was established in his area over 20 years ago. In Delaware a man served as treasurer for 20 years. In central Ohio the school board term is generally 3 years, in Indiana 6 years. The man who has served the longest acts as president. He can usually expect to be off the board for one year between terms. Work as a school board member takes a great deal of time, energy, and personal skill, so a year of rest is generally appreciated. Church officials, who are often busy with church responsibilities, are rarely elected to school boards; however, in a few instances they do serve as teachers.

The school board hires and fires the teacher, pays the salary, enforces attendance laws, supplies the equipment needed by the school, and keeps the building and playground in good condition. It sets the tuition fee and levies or assesses the school tax against those who have elected it. The school board meets as a unit with the teacher, ideally once a month. These are open meetings and parents and other church members are encouraged to attend. The school board is responsible to the patrons, which usually also means the local church district, for the smooth functioning of the school.

Statewide Amish board meetings are held annually for members of the school boards, committeemen, and other interested church members. Officers are elected by a vote of those present at the meeting. Pennsylvania has held annual meetings since 1957, Ohio since about 1958, and Indiana since 1964. Within these three states, which have the largest Amish populations, there were statewide meetings at earlier dates. The Amish Church School Committee (of Pennsylvania) was established in 1937. Through the years it attempted to clarify the Amish position on education to state education officials. When a new state board was set up in Indiana, the ministers and men of the districts that were operating schools were eligible to vote. Continuity is extremely important on these state committees, and most of the officers serve for a long time.

The state committee has several subcommittees. A small executive committee works directly with public education officials to make necessary adjustments between the state department of public education and the Amish schools. These committeemen also meet with Amish in other areas who are contemplating establishing a school. A Pennsylvania subcommittee, the Old Order Book Society, is made up of both members and nonmembers of the state board. The original function of the society was to find and, if necessary, print books suitable for use in Amish schools. This committee also functions as a state treasury to help provide funds for the establishment of new community schools. Indiana has both a book and curriculum committee and a treasury committee. The treasury committee works on the funding of new schools. The curriculum committee is working towards uniform curricula for the Amish schools in the state. The Ohio Amish have a less-developed state organization. Their chief spokesman pointed out to the Amish School Study Committee of the Department of Education that "Amish schools like Amish churches are self-governing units. Lack of centralization is important to both" (Ohio Legislative Service Commission 1960:20). The Ohio Amish school standards drawn up by the state Delegative Committee has been used in Indiana and Wisconsin to help in getting state recognition for Amish schools.

Because the organization of the Amish school system is relatively fluid, it is difficult to generalize about its financial basis. One Amishman in Pennsylvania commented, "There are eight or nine different [school] boards or districts here in Lancaster county, and only a few have the same way of collecting funds." Financial requirements are of two basically different types: (1) building or establishing a new school, and (2) running an established school. Different methods are often used to obtain funds for these two categories of expenses.

The land is often donated for the school; money for the new school may have been raised by free-will donations, by taxing the Amish church members according to their property evaluation, by assessing each family head or each member a specified amount, or by any combination of these plans. Or the money may all be supplied by shareholders in the schools, in which case a part may have been borrowed (often interest-free) from church members. The building may be owned by the church district, by a few parents, or by a single individual. Generally the materials are bought and the labor is supplied free of charge by the community.

Even with the large amount of donated labor, Amish schools today usually cost between $5,000 and $10,000 to build. There is a growing tendency for the schools to be financed by the whole church, rather than by a group of parents. In this way the financial base is enlarged. Thus, church districts are grouping together to support their schools. At first these groupings included neighboring areas, then whole Amish communities; now there is an effort to have most of the cost of the new schools borne by all the Amish of a single affiliation within the whole state. Various settlements in Ohio each have their own methods for financing new schools rather than a statewide organization; money needed in excess of that provided by the cluster of church districts is supplied by the local Amish school board. As enthusiasm for Amish community schools gains momentum there is a growing consensus that all Amishmen, whether or not they have children in Amish schools, should contribute to the support of these schools.

The operating expenses as well as the initial building expenses for the Amish schools are obtained in a variety of ways: free-will offerings by church members, assessment according to real estate evaluation combined with individual member assessment, and tuition. Often these methods are combined. If the school is owned by only some of the parents, then different tuition is charged to those who do not own a share. Tuition may run as high as $18 per month, but it is never used as the exclusive method of financing.

The tuition system is described by a teacher in a community where is is used: "Each church member of both the north and south church districts is to pay $5 annually for coal, repairs, and books. Any money left was put on the debt, and as that is now paid, the balance goes to help pay the teachers. Only those parents having children in school pay tuition, and it is the same for each family, no matter how many or how few scholars each has. Any orphan children's or needy family's tuition is paid out of the church treasury."

An assessment system of support is described by a parent: "When money is needed, the treasurer sends word to the various church districts, and the fact is announced in church, and how much is needed. Usually it is $5 per church member as often as may be needed. In the fall, and again around New Year, a collection is taken that is figured on the assessed property valuation." This system is the most widely used among the Amish, but the ease with which it is administered varies greatly from one district to another. Some encouragement is necessary for those members who are slow or reluctant in paying. In urging his co-religionists to help finance the schools, one Amish person pointed out, "You can't take your property to heaven with you—but you can take your children."

Most Amish schools are built efficiently, with a great deal of the labor and even materials being donated. All the janitorial care and incidental labor on the building and grounds are given freely. The physical plant is simple, with a low upkeep cost. The dedicated teachers serve willingly for relatively low wages. During the school year 1965–66, the 13 Amish schools in one county with a pupil enrollment of 599 spent $24,087.21 on the twenty teachers' salaries and on running expenses. Although this was considered expensive by the Amish, it is by comparison with most public schools systems very economical. During the 1966–67 academic year an average of $55 was spent in the public school to instruct each grammar school pupil (Sava 1968:102). In other words, if the 599 Amish children had been educated in the public schools, it would have cost $272,545 instead of $24,087 for the same period. A parent from Maryland pointed out that the Amish schools there operate on the amount of money it had cost the county the previous year just to transport the Amish children to the public school.

PHYSICAL SETTING

Most Old Order Amish school buildings consist of one or two classrooms, often with an entrance room, sometimes a bookroom, and in the newer schools with a finished basement where the children play during inclement weather. Rural one- and two-room schoolhouses are purchased from the state when they are available, moved if necessary, and often extensively remodeled. The Amish dislike the high ceilings typical of state buildings, so they often lower the ceiling to create a cosier, more homelike atmosphere. Most often no old schoolhouses are available, and they build their own. The schools are well built, of glazed tile, cinder block, brick facing, stucco, or aluminum siding. They are built in such a way as to take full advantage of available natural light, for Amish schools do not have electricity.

Many Amish schoolhouses have old-fashioned, rope-pulled school bells. Doors open outward; the buildings are insulated and properly ventilated, and materials that can easily be kept clean are used throughout the schools. Schools in certain communities have indoor lavatories, but in most areas outhouses are preferred. The Amish building committees have their blueprints approved by the state officials and work closely with the health officers of the state "who know better than we do how a school should be designed" (Stoll 1965:61). The same set of blueprints may be used for more than one school. One-room schools usually range from 24 to 30 feet by 34 to 48 feet. If the terrain is suitable, the building is set true with the directions of the compass, for this helps the children learn directional orientation. In Kishacoquillas Valley in Pennsylvania all the schools are built with the teacher's desk and blackboards at the north end of the building because then "when the children face north to study maps, the lay of the county and the land will be imprinted in their minds exactly as it is." The Amish schoolhouses do not have the grace of early Shaker buildings, but they are simple, sensible, serviceable, and well built of good quality material.

The site of the school is carefully considered. Ideally the school is located on a well drained parcel of land that provides a large, safe play area for the children. If possible, it is located in such a way that all the pupils can walk to school. However,

Amish schoolhouses. Top: Ohio. Bottom: Pennsylvania.

quite a few schools build small barns for the horses of children who come to school by buggy, and in Pennsylvania and Indiana some of the children ride to school on school buses. Every school has a ballfield; some have as many as three baseball diamonds. Only a few schools have swings or seesaws, but activities such as sledding and ice skating are considered when choosing a location. The parents graded the land at one school to build a sledding area for the children.

Typically an Amish school is entered through a cloakroom in which the children hang their hats, jackets, bonnets, and shawls, and store their boots and lunch buckets. The girls use one side of the room; the boys, the other. In some of the newer schools, wraps are hung in the basement. The main classroom is usually entered at the back of the room. The teacher's desk is at the front, as is a recitation bench. Along the front wall is a large chalkboard, above which are the alphabet and the children's names and grades on decorated posters. Along the side walls are large windows and either bulletin boards or chalkboards. In schools with cinder block or tile walls, all the walls are used as bulletin boards. The amount of decoration is determined by the personality and interests of the teacher and by the board that controls the school. The most conservative church districts allow almost no decoration. Only the children's names, ages, and grades, and such things as a calendar and spelling charts and perhaps a few mottoes are permitted. Compared to many Hutterite schools (Hostetler and Huntington 1967:67–73), where nothing is permitted to be hung on the walls or left on the top of the teacher's desk or table after a school day, even these classrooms appear to be decorated.

In most Amish schools colorful pictures and charts are on both the walls and windows, but the rooms are never cluttered. The impression is one of lightness, brightness, and order. Most often the desks and chairs have been bought from old public schools and refinished. They are smooth and shiny, although they probably date from before World War I. The desks are screwed to strips of wood, four to a plank, so that the room can be rearranged, but the desks will not easily get out of line. Most teachers prefer these to individual desks for the children.

The large majority of Amish schools have only one room. Some are designed so that a second classroom can be added on. Two-room school houses may be built with a movable partition that enables the rooms to be opened up for meetings and large gatherings. Occasionally, two teachers will teach in one large classroom, but this has obvious disadvantages. It seems to work most successfully when the teachers are husband and wife or two sisters who naturally team-teach.

SCHEDULE

All Amish schools follow the same basic schedule, and it is virtually identical with that followed in the one-room rural schools of 50 years ago. The day is divided up into four major periods of approximately an hour and a half each. Between each period is a recess or the noon break. During each period the various classes recite; generally about 10 minutes is allowed for each class recitation. The children who are not reciting know when it will be their turn and what subject they should be studying. Questions from students in their seats are answered between classes, but rarely during recitation.

Most Amish schools start at 8:30 or 9:00 and finish between 3:30 and 4:30 in the afternoon. There are 15-minute recesses in the middle of the morning and the middle of the afternoon and an hour break for lunch in the middle of the day.

Often the teacher schedules the subject she believes to be the hardest or the most important for the first hour. Some schools have reading first, some arithmetic. Spelling, generally considered an easy subject, is usually scheduled late in the afternoon, as are art or handicrafts, if the school has these, or various educational games or special projects.

All schools have an opening period that includes singing hymns, often in both English and German. Whether these opening exercises are in English or German or both depends largely upon the community. Many schools recite prayers, usually the Lord's Prayer. In schools where the Bible is read during the opening exercises, students may read the selection from the Sunday church service in order to tie the school and church more closely together. Many schools have a song before dismissing for lunch, and some recite a noon prayer. Teachers may read to the children for a few minutes at the beginning of the afternoon session, occasionally from a completely secular book like a Nancy Drew mystery. Children often sing one or more songs before the afternoon dismissal, and some sing as they file out of their seats to put on their wraps.

Although musical notation is not taught, singing is very important in Amish schools, and teachers are always interested in learning new songs and ways to encourage children to enjoy singing. Not only do children learn many hymns, but

Recitation class (Photo by Vincent R. Tortora).

in some schools they also learn to lead songs according to the Amish tradition. The teacher sings the first note or two of each line and then the rest join in. All singing, except rounds, is in unison. Pupils who visit neighboring schools always sing together. The teachers, too, sing at their gatherings.

CURRICULUM

The slight variation in curricula of Amish elementary schools is determined by local preferences and different state education department rulings on private school curricula. Basically the children learn English (including reading, grammar, spelling, penmanship, and to a limited extent, composition) and arithmetic (adding, subtracting, multiplying, decimals, dividing, percentages, ratios, volumes and areas, conversion of weights and measures, and simple and compound interest). New math is not taught. Most schools teach some health, history, and geography; some teach a little science and art. Some very conservative Old Order Amish community schools substitute agriculture for history and geography. Reading is taught by the phonetic method; the children learn their letters and sounds before they begin reading. In grammar they learn the parts of speech and the rules of usage.

The textbooks used are determined by the school board, with or without consultation with the teacher. Pennsylvania and Indiana have statewide committees to help with the selection of books. The Old Order Amish Book Society publishes a list of books suitable for Amish schools. Various textbooks are discussed in the *Blackboard Bulletin* (a teacher's journal), at teachers' meetings, and informally by teachers whenever they meet. When a school first opens, it may use whatever textbooks are available. In one instance the families brought in all the textbooks they owned, and from these enough were gathered for the school. In other areas local public school teachers and administrators have been generous in donating discarded books to the Amish school, and in other cases older books have been purchased at reduced prices. Older texts may be preferred because they are familiar; they have been used by parents and other community members and thus represent shared knowledge. They may be preferred because less science and fewer modern developments, such as television, are incorporated into the stories. The pictures are also considered less offensive. The Amish are opposed to any sex education in school and to the type of health books that stress popularity and how to make oneself attractive. The Amish teach their children that they should adjust to others and not expect others to adjust to them, that one should not be concerned with how he can influence others, but rather how he can serve them.

Various Amish schools use the *Alice and Jerry* series, the *Dick and Jane* series, the *Scott-Foresman New Basic Readers*, the *Golden Rule* series (also known as "The New McGuffy Readers"), and the original *McGuffey's Readers*. More teachers than parents like the *Alice and Jerry* books. The teachers like to teach reading from them, but the parents show some concern with their worldliness and play orientation, "their meaningless prattle, their TV stories, and their pictures of children in bathing suits." Jules Henry (1969:86) has pointed out that the illustrations in the

Dick and Jane series subtly support conspicuous consumption; in a succession of stories "the entire family is wearing a different and attractive set of clothes." The stories in the *Golden Rule* series all have a moral, but many of these are superficially patriotic or militaristic and are not really appropriate for a nonresistant group that tries to live "separated from the world." The Old Order Amish Book Society recommends the *Scott-Foresman New Basic Readers* for the first four grades. They recommend using a phonics book, for example, *Reading with Phonics* (J. B. Lippincott Company). Other teachers recommend the phono-visual method.

The wide use of *McGuffey Readers* in Ohio is not surprising, because they were written by one of the founders of the common school system in Ohio at a time when the "notion that education itself was primarily moral, and only secondarily intellectual . . ." and "that the primary business of schools was to train character" was held throughout America (Commager 1962:viii). This idea of education, of course, coincides with the Amish attitude. Even the brand of patriotism expounded in the *McGuffey Readers* is shared by the Amish, for it is a "pride in the virtues and the beauties of the nation, not in its prowess or its superiority to other nations"

Children cleaning their shoes before entering the schoolhouse (Photo by Charles S. Rice).

(Commager 1963:xv). Just as the *McGuffey Readers* functioned during the mid-nineteenth century to produce a common body of allusion and a common frame of reference among most Americans, so these readers still function today among the Amish in Ohio and to a much lesser degree among the Amish in other states.

Some of the teachers do not like the *McGuffey Readers* as much as the parents do. They complain that though many of the stories are good, the vocabulary is difficult and outdated and much of the material is not very meaningful to the children. The editor of the *Blackboard Bulletin* made a more basic criticism of these and other readers of the mid-nineteenth century. He noted that though the stories were highly moral in tone, the moralism was often worldly and materialistic. Of these stories he says, "First, they are not real to life. Good little boys just aren't rewarded with pocket knives and gold coins every time they overcome a temptation and do what is right. And I for one don't want my children brought up to expect a reward for doing good. Secondly, in most of the old stories the reward is a material one. This is wrong, it seems to me. The reward for virtue should never be a matter of dollars and cents. If there is a reward, it is a spiritual one first of all." (*Blackboard Bulletin*, May 1969:207).

Due to the difficulty of finding good reading books for their schools, The Pathway Publishers, an Old Order Amish publishing house, has undertaken the task of producing readers for the upper grades, five through eight (Pathway Reading Series 1968). The Amish do not want their children to read fairy tales or myths; many object to any stories that are not true, such as those in which animals talk and act like people or stories that involve magic, such as "The Pied Piper of Hamlin." The stories must not glorify physical force, nationalism, militarism, or modern technology. The subject matter should be American and rural if possible, for stories of distant countries and other cultures have little relevance for these children. Each story should teach a moral; those that are "just nice" are not good enough. It is difficult to find well-written stories suitable for grades five, six, seven, and eight that meet all these requirements. In the Pathway Series some stories are of Amish authorship. The stories and poems teach moral values and Christian virtues of honesty, thrift, purity, and love—without undue religiosity. Some selections are also designed to help children appreciate nature and a rural way of life.

A variety of books from different publishing houses are used to teach English language skills. Penmanship is taught in all the schools. Some use the *Penmanship Pad* printed by the Old Order Book Society in Pennsylvania. As the public schools change textbooks from traditional arithmetic to new math, the Amish schools are sometimes able to obtain the old books. The most widely used arithmetic books are the *Strayer Upton Practical Arithmetic* series published by the American Book Company. The Laidlow health series is used in many schools. The children in grades five through eight study American history and geography and world history and geography. A variety of different books are used, depending on what is available.

The Amish have published two history books that are used in some elementary schools and in schools that teach ninth grade. These books were printed for and distributed by the Old Order Book Society. They are *Seeking a Better Country*

(1963) by Noah Zook and *Our Better Country, The Story of America's Freedom* (1963) by Uria R. Byler. Both include a fair amount of Amish history and help the children to understand their relation to secular history. One Amish author points out that the children should be taught that the early framers of the constitution worked long and carefully to protect the individual and the religious rights of future American citizens and that they began and ended each of their working sessions with a prayer. The children should know the full meaning of the efforts of these deeply concerned men, since they protect Amishmen in their practice of religion and in their right to attend their own schools (Byler 1963).

In their community schools the Amish children are presented with certain appropriate facts, which they are encouraged to learn thoroughly rather than to question critically. These basic facts form a part of their shared knowledge and thus help the community remain of one mind, so decisions can be made from a common core of knowledge. Amish pupils are taught correct answers. Even if there is a range of possible alternatives, children are generally taught that one of the possibilities "is right for you." This is consistent with the church's deciding as a unit what rules will be applicable and what behavior is correct in each church district.

What is omitted from the Amish school curriculum is as important as what is taught, for the school functions as one of the boundary-maintaining mechanisms for the culture, keeping the children sheltered from "the world." Most Old Order Amish attribute a positive teaching role to their schools, but a few conservative Old Order affiliations see the role of the school as primarily negative, its function being to remove unnecessary and dangerous facts from the children's environment. These churches do not want either geography or history to be taught, for both subjects present the outside world with its wars, intrigues, and technology.

Ideally the curriculum of the Amish elementary school helps the child to live his Christianity and thus eventually to achieve not historical or earthly acclaim, but eternal rewards. The child learns not to be overly concerned with his place in the world but to concentrate on preparation for eternity. He is told, "Do all the good you can, but do not feel important; this world would be here anyhow, even if you and I had never been born."

LANGUAGE ROLES

In addition to the basic academic subjects, most but not all the Amish elementary schools teach German. Before the Amish had their own schools and still attended public schools, they often had supplementary German classes to help the children master High German so that they could read the German Bible. The Amish do not speak High German but Pennsylvania Dutch, which functions effectively to maintain the boundary between the Amish and the outside world. The relationship between English (the language of the world), German (the language of the Bible), and Pennsylvania Dutch (the language of the home) is a subject of concern in many Amish communities. Pennsylvania Dutch is the preferred spoken language and is used exclusively within the household and community; it is the family's responsibility to give its children a firm foundation in the mother tongue. In addition, the children must learn to speak, read, and write English to live successfully on the margin of the twentieth century; it is the responsibility of the school to teach the children English. There is complete agreement among the Amish that only English should be spoken during all school hours except for actual German classes. But there is disagreement as to whether English or Pennsylvania Dutch should be spoken on the playground. The majority of schools encourage the use of English during recess, for the teachers believe it helps the children become fluent in English. However, some parents fear that the children are becoming too fluent in English and are preferring it to Pennsylvania Dutch.

In order to understand the strong feelings aroused by discussions of whether or not to allow Pennsylvania Dutch to be spoken on the playground, and of how much time should be devoted to studying High German, it is necessary to know what English and German represent to most Amishmen. Joseph Stoll explains it well:

> As Old Order Amish, we associate German with church services and our home life—the religious and deeply moral part of our lives. German in a sense represents all that we have for centuries been trying to hold—our heritage as a nonconformed people, pilgrims in an alien land. It represents the old, the tried, and proven, the sacred way.
>
> The English language, by contrast, we associate with the business world, society, worldliness. English in a sense represents everything outside our church and community, the forces that have become dangerous because they make inroads into our churches and lure people from the faith. Therefore, the English language, though acknowledged all right in its place, becomes suspect when associated with the lure of the world (*Blackboard Bulletin*, May 1969:208).

Due to the close tie between the German language and religion in the minds of the Amish and to their history of learning German outside the schools, some communities still have members come into the school to teach German. Often one of the respected men in the community will teach German half a day a week. However, as the total community emotionally accepts the school as an integral part of it, the regular schoolteacher is taking over the role of German teacher. In no school is High German taught as a means of oral communication. All oral discussion is in Pennsylvania Dutch. Though they do not know how to converse in High German, most graduates of Amish elementary schools are expected to be able to read the Bible aloud in High German and to love its cadence even though they may not fully understand the exact meaning of each word. High German is more than just another language to the Amish. It is the basis of their sermons and ceremonies, their religious oral tradition, and their collective memory and wisdom.

RELIGIOUS EDUCATION

The Amish school supports the religion taught in the family and in the community but is not an interpreter of religious doctrine. There is a strong feeling among the Amish that only the ordained, who have been called by God, should explain the Scriptures to an assembled group. Within the family the parents teach their own children but not other people's children. The points of difference between affiliations are so slight that it is difficult for anyone not directly involved to understand them, yet they can be of great concern to Amish individuals. Disagreement on small points of doctrine or application can lead to dissension. Intellectual discussion and argued interpretation of the Bible may, therefore, be dangerous to community solidarity. At informal gatherings people will talk about the Bible and refer to it, but in traditional Amish circles classes for Bible study are not acceptable, either within the community or within the school. The Bible used didactically, rather than ritualistically, is inflammatory.

The relation of the school to religious education is symbolized in a diagram (on the cover of the *Blackboard Bulletin*, January 1953) showing education, religion, and morality conjoined, with the statement: "The constant aim of our schools is to fuse morality, religion, and education into one broad goal. The goal is to teach children to live that they may have eternal Life." Religion is central to the Amish way of life—the foundation of their morality and their secular education. Because "Christianity pervades all of life, it will come out in all subjects in school" and therefore does not have to be taught as a separate subject.

The Old Order Amish Christianity is primarily ritualistic and nontheological. Christianity for them must be lived, not talked. They are critical of the person who shows off his knowledge of scripture by frequently quoting passages. This is considered a form of pride, and pride in any form is despicable. Teachers are "advised not to include Sunday School lessons, nor induce the child to be Scripture-smart for religious show." In Amish schools Bible verses can be memorized and German can be learned from the New Testament, for like the singing of hymns, this is part of the ritual of the oral tradition of the Amish. It represents shared experience rather than intellectual analysis. In the same way, reading the Bible without comment, reading a Bible story during opening exercises, or the recitation of the Lord's prayer in unison are of this tradition.

All the Old Order Amish, even those who believe that the Bible should be studied in school, believe that Christianity is better taught by example than by lecture. "We can teach the Bible in our schools," said one Amishman, "but . . . if the Bible principles of love, forebearing, humility, and self-denial aren't practiced by parents and teachers, then I don't see where any Bible teaching in the school will have too much effect. A child will learn 10 times as fast if the Christianity he is taught is also practiced than he will by merely being told how to practice it." Another typical attitude is expressed in a teacher's statement: "Reading from the Bible in school is necessary, but many feel that explaining the meaning should be left to someone else. We teachers could misinform the children." If the teacher is a woman, her status as a woman is a further reason for her not to expound the Scriptures.

The New or emergent Amish tend to intellectualize religion: "What Bible verse is applicable to the way I feel?" "Can I find the verse to tell me what I should do next?" In such groups the school also gives religion a great deal more verbal emphasis. But among the traditional Amish, religious expression is less self-conscious; because it gives an overall direction to life, small signposts are not needed at every crossroads. The traditional Amish are attempting to keep this orientation, but because their position is not intellectualized it is difficult to define logically, especially to those who are facile in quoting the Bible. This places the traditional Amish at a disadvantage when they must defend their position verbally. Realizing all too well this disadvantage, some Amishmen feel that they must be equipped to demonstrate their Christianity on all fronts and therefore that they must study the Bible intellectually, as well as learning it ritualistically. This feeling is more prevalent in the less traditional communities, for they are the ones who have greater contact outside their own community and consequently are more aware of their lack of training in intellectual argument.

EXTRACURRICULAR LEARNING

Amish pupils learn many things at their school that are not strictly part of the curriculum, but that help them to become well socialized members of the larger community. Amish visitors are always welcomed at the school. The children are

Schoolgirls cleaning the blackboard erasers (Photo by Charles S. Rice).

quietly pleased to have visitors, the teacher greets them and introduces them to the children, telling not only who they are but where they come from. Usually the visitors say a few words to the children, and the children sing some songs for the guests. The children enjoy this interaction with the wider community and appreciate adults coming to their school. The children often learn something of other Amish communities, for the guests may be parents or neighbors or may be from out of state. Not only do adults come, but vocational students, recent graduates, and seventh- and eighth-grade pupils from other schools visit, adding to the network of relationships within the wider community. Schools exchange letters, and children have pen pals in other communities whom one day they will meet. Some schools publish papers that they take home to their families and exchange with other schools. When someone in the neighborhood is ill, the children write letters and perhaps make a scrapbook for the shut-in. They will visit and sing for an elderly neighbor who is housebound. All these activities help the children to learn their responsibilities and understand their place in the wider Amish community.

The janitorial work is done by the teacher and the children. They tend the heating stove, bring in the wood or coal, pick up litter from the yard, and keep the schoolroom swept. It is their school. Their parents paid for it; they built it with their own hands, and the children and their teacher keep it warm, clean, and neat. This care and involvement helps to produce a strong tie of affection.

The children bring sandwiches to school, which they may heat on the stove and eat at their desks during the first 10 or 15 minutes of the noon hour. The rest of the hour they are free. When the weather is pleasant they play vigorously in the schoolyard, but during the winter there is a long time to spend inside. Schools with finished basements have lively games of various types, such as dodgeball or ping-pong games with as many as 20 children playing at once circling the table, each with his own table tennis paddle. They may play pussy-in-the-corner, hopscotch, red light, fruit basket, or blindman's buff. They also play such board games as parchesi, checkers, Chinese checkers, Sorry, and carrom. Jacks and marbles are popular, and in some schools children play dominos and educational lotto. They also put together puzzles and play chalk games at the blackboard. The youngest ones like to play school. Outside in good weather, if there is play equipment such as swings, seesaws, and basketball hoops, these are popular; but nothing is as well liked, especially by the older children, as softball. When there is snow, they sled and play fox and geese. Other popular games are prisoner's base, grey wolf, kick-the-can, Red Rover, Andy-over, follow-the-leader, and a variety of tag games. Children are encouraged to play as a group; they are not permitted to leave two or three children standing around, nor are they allowed to exclude one another from their talk or play. Some teachers use the winter noon hour to teach the girls to knit, crochet, or embroider. In good weather the teachers go outside with the children and often join in the games with them.

Teachers take their students on trips. They may take small walks into the woods to observe the fall colors and enjoy a picnic or they may go by haywagon to a neighboring farm to eat their lunch and watch the well-drillers. Sometimes the children in the upper grades go by horse and buggy with their teachers to visit other Amish schools, while the younger children are taught by a substitute. In some areas it is the custom at the end of the school year to take the seventh- and eighth-grade students on a trip. These trips last only one day, but it is not unusual for the day to begin at 5 in the morning, end after 10 at night, and involve hundreds of miles of driving. One such year-end trip includes stops at points of national historic interest, places of interest to the Amish, the airport, several small factories producing food products, an egg-grading plant, and the agricultural experiment station. Sometimes they go to the state capitol, or they may visit a hospital. They always stop at a city store and have about 45 minutes to look around and shop for souvenirs. The pupils learn a great deal on these trips, and they are long remembered as very special days.

Such teacher-pupil activity in extracurricular learning is not only rewarding to individuals but the shared experiences help make the school "an intensified part of life" (Dennison 1969:33) and an integral part of a culture that is supremely social.

THE PROBLEM SCHOOL

Every school system has its problem schools, and the Amish are no exception. They are the first to say that some of their schools are "not what we would like them to be." What problems do the Amish have with their schools and what factors produce problems?

Amish schools are community schools, so any disintegration in the community is reflected in the school. A division within the community makes it more difficult for the teacher to have a school characterized by warmth and unity; cliques may develop among the children. The financial backing for the school is likely to be more precarious in a community that is not of one mind. In such a community the teacher usually does not enjoy the needed emotional and social support. Small settlements, geographically separated from larger ones, may have more trouble securing teachers; and the teachers, being somewhat isolated from other teachers, receive less help and support from their peers. Sometimes this leads not necessarily to poor schools, but to schools characterized by less variety of experience and less enthusiasm on the part of both the teacher and the pupils. Some of the smaller communities have less to offer the school in all areas of educational support. On the other hand, the new, small community may make up with commitment and zeal for its lack of members and relative isolation from other Amish. There is variation among communities in their attitude towards the physical plant of the school. A poorly maintained school, one that needs painting and perhaps land-scaping, has more of an adverse effect on public opinion (non-Amish) than it does on the quality of the education the children receive. Schools that look quite dreary on the outside may be bright and lively inside. A few schools are run-down inside and out. A school board that is not highly motivated and unwilling to contribute time and energy is likely to have a poorer school to administer. A strong teacher and a few dedicated parents may successfully counteract a weak school board.

Occasionally a school will be plagued with a high rate of teacher turnover. This invariably has an unfortunate effect on the children and makes it still more difficult to find a good teacher who can work with the children to build a good school. The quality of the teacher is crucial to the quality of the school, but even a good teacher can be undermined by lack of community support. There is considerable variation in the intelligence, skill, imagination, and dedication of different teachers. However, individuals who are clearly unsuited for teaching do not teach long in an Amish community. Very young teachers are more likely to have trouble than older teachers, especially in the area of discipline. One of the early symptoms of trouble is disrespect and poor discipline. There does not seem to be a difference between men and women teachers in relation to the quality of the school. A school that has become a problem due to poor teaching is relatively easily corrected; one that has become a problem school because of community disorganization is much more difficult to deal with.

Problem parents can undermine a good school. On a somewhat superficial level this type of parent does not help his children to get to school on time. A more serious problem arises if parents keep children at home when they should be in school. If a parent is uncooperative to the extent of keeping his child at home to work, then that child is transferred to the public school and comes under their legal jurisdiction. However, this is almost never necessary, for community pressure and reasonable persuasion is generally sufficient to keep a good attendance record. Occasionally parents may undermine the teacher's authority and contribute to dissension in the school. A basically healthy community and a school with a good board can generally absorb a few such parents without undue harm to the school.

The Amish are competent judges of what is a good school and what is a poor school. They are aware of the factors that contribute to both and are constantly working for improvement. In an effort to determine whether it is possible for the Old Order Amish to provide an adequate formal education for their children, we selected schools for intensive study that were judged good by the Amish themselves. We were interested in the validity of their evaluation as well as in appraising their ability to provide a good education for their children. At this stage we were not undertaking a survey of the schools nor even a constructed cross section. The Amish school movement is so new that we were interested more in the direction towards which they were working than in making a total evaluation. We were impressed with how well these schools functioned and how few serious problems arose. We also observed, although we did not test, in problem schools. We noted how problems were assessed by the Amish and how steps were taken that lead to improvement. Because the school unit is small and the communities cohesive, problem schools can become good schools relatively quickly; and conversely, with the advent of a poor teacher, they can also deteriorate rapidly. As the Amish schools become better established, they appear to be improving in their ability to provide a good education for the children they serve.

4/The Amish
elementary school teacher

QUALIFICATIONS

WHEN COUNTY SCHOOL superintendents initially learn that Amish teachers have no formal training beyond eighth grade, they are often appalled and doubt the teachers' qualifications. But to the Amish, qualifications for teaching have little relation to the acquisition of college degrees. Qualifications and suitability for teaching in Amish society are best understood by comparing the role of teacher in the two cultures, the Amish and the typical suburban school.

Today in many suburban schools, by the time children have reached fifth grade they know more about certain facts and even areas of knowledge than a teacher who must teach all subjects. The prevalence of television, ease of travel, and the availability of books stimulate children's curiosity and enable many of them to pursue their interests, at least in limited areas, to a remarkable degree. The American school system emphasizes the development of the students' rational powers. The amount of factual material that children are taught steadily increases as the total amount of knowledge increases and as society becomes more complex. For these reasons, it is essential that public school teachers be well trained.

Outside the classroom, the public school teacher disappears from the life of his pupils. They do not know how he spends his time, what he does, how he lives, or what he believes about religion or politics—and these may, in fact, have surprisingly little influence on the subject matter he teaches the children. The public school teacher must be competent in his subject and able in his teaching methods, for, at least superficially, he is hired to teach technology rather than wisdom. Most communities do not want him to teach attitudes or beliefs, other than belief in the scientific method and our form of government. They want him to stick to his subject: teach the children the material, but not how in a moral sense the material should be used. The teacher is an authority on subject matter; his authority comes from his training; and most of that comes from books. The printed word—the most recently printed word—is the final authority in most American classrooms.

The Amish, who have kept radio, television, and movies outside their experience, have been minimally affected by the communications revolution. They have limited

Schoolroom scene (Photo by Vincent R. Tortora).

the printed word, rejecting much of the more recent material that flows from the world's printing presses. In maintaining a primitive type of Christian church, they have kept an oral tradition and an orientation to life that is relational rather than analytical (Cohen 1969). By its very nature oral tradition is social; it is tied to the community. Where there is extreme reliance on the printed word, teacher and pupil need never meet. In contrast, the oral tradition requires personal interaction; teaching within this tradition is by example as well as by word.

In keeping with the oral tradition, the Amish teacher must teach with his whole life. He should be a person integrated within himself and integrated with the community, for every aspect of his behavior and of his personality is related to his teaching. He must be well grounded in his religious faith and completely committed to the Amish way of life, accepting the limits set by the *Ordnung* and exemplifying the Amish traits of humility, obedience, steadfastness, and love for his fellow man. In addition, he must be interested in education and have sufficient factual knowledge to provide a substantial margin between him and his students. In other words, the teachers should be capable and sound of character.

An elderly teacher explains the Amish attitude toward qualification and certification: "It is essential that we have qualified teachers. By that I do not mean certified ones, for state-certified teachers do not qualify for teaching in our schools." State certified teachers are not qualified because their approach is mainly cerebral (understanding-oriented) rather than visceral (identification-oriented), to use a distinction made by Saltzman (1963:323) in discussing successful community schools. Both qualities are essential to cultural integrity and continuity. Teachers who understand but do not identify with the community are at a serious disadvantage when they confront children and parents who differ from them in race, class, culture, or ethnicity. Trained middle-class teachers are too far removed from the oral tradition to identify with the Amish, and in most instances they are unsuitable as examples.

Because the Amish teachers' role is primarily that of Christian example rather than authority in subject matter or methodology, they are not likely to present themselves to the children as "gods, all-knowing, all-powerful, always rational, always just, always right" (Holt 1964:171). Instead they freely admit their human weaknesses and the need to turn to the "Master Teacher" for help and guidance.

The Amish regard teaching with such importance that it is beginning to be thought of as a calling rather than a job. Their ministers are called; that is, they do not themselves choose to be ministers, but are chosen by the congregation of God through the working of the lot. Similarly, an Amish person usually does not apply for his first teaching job; rather he is approached by the school board. One girl said they had "been after" her for about six years before she decided she was ready to teach. When she did decide, she spent several weeks with various good teachers in the area, observing and helping for a week in each school. If the prospective teacher is younger than 21, the father is asked, rather than the girl or boy directly, since an Amishman is under the care of his father socially and financially until he is 21. One young teacher who had enjoyed her year of teaching said she was trying to persuade her father to let her teach next year, "but I can bring so much more money home if I clean house and baby-sit and we don't have much money, so that maybe I'll have to do housework instead." In such a case the school board may try to remind the father how important it is to have good teachers in the Amish school. Teachers who have taught successfully are believed to have demonstrated that they have a calling, and if they wish to change jobs, they can apply to another school. However, the teachers' grapevine is sufficiently effective that the information is usually passed around informally, enabling the school board to make the initial move. A good teacher may receive as many as six or seven requests, even if she has not indicated an interest in changing schools. These requests are written in such a way that they are very difficult to turn down. The relationship between teacher and school board, both by letter and when the school board calls, is a very personal one and does not in any way resemble a business agreement.

Amish teachers are not motivated by monetary rewards. They do not have contracts, nor do they have tenure. Life is uncertain, and no one knows when it will change. Perhaps the teacher will be needed somewhere else. If her parents fall sick, for instance, she may have to stop teaching to care for them; or a young man who has been teaching may have to stop to take over his father's farm. The same principle applies if the teacher turns out to be unsuccessful. He or she is asked to leave. This is considered unfortunate, for it is hard on the children. If a teacher, however, can not handle the work, it is obvious that God did not intend for him to teach and that it would be better for everyone for him to do something else. The Amishman who remains a teacher does so because he has demonstrated talent and because generally he wants to teach.

TEACHING METHODS AND SCHOOL MANAGEMENT

An Amish teacher's way of life and his teaching methods are in agreement. He teaches primarily by being an exemplary individual in close contact with the children. The teacher is a role model. But he is more than a role model, for he also imparts facts as well as his attitudes and his beliefs as to how these facts should be used and how they fit into an Amish world view. He creates the atmosphere of the school. He is the shepherd, the responsible adult, who is older and more experienced and knows better than the children what is good for them. The classroom runs smoothly, for he does not pretend that the children make the decisions. An Amish teacher quietly tells a child what to do and he does it. Obedience and order are basic to a good school not just part of the time but all of the time. A biblical phrase, "Let everything be done decently and in order" (I Corinthians 14:40), is a motto on the wall of some classrooms. "For God is not the author of confusion, but of peace" (I Corinthians 14:33) is recited by the pupils. Orderliness is believed to make for more security and less tension in the pupils' lives.

Amish teachers instruct their children to "Do unto others, as you would have others do unto you." This quotation "should be placed in front of the schoolroom where all children can see and study it, and the teacher should quite often point to it as a reminder that this Golden Rule should be followed at all times" (Byler 1969). The Golden Rule is not compatible with individualistic competition. The Amish teach a nonexploitive value system by emphasizing individual responsibility rather than self-assertiveness. The Amish schools avoid the contradiction that Jules Henry (1963:295–297) speaks of in many modern public schools, where the children are simultaneously taught to compete and to have love for one another. There is some competition in the Amish schools, but it is usually structured to support the group. The children will try to have better attendance this week than last week, better spelling scores this month than last month. They may even vie with another school for good attendance, or the teacher may post weekly spelling scores from a school where she taught some years ago and the children as a school, or as a class, try to do better than her former pupils. Under the teacher's guidance the peer group is used to enhance adult values. The children encourage one another's good performance in order that their whole class or their school may do well (Bronfenbrenner 1970:50).

The Amish believe that an individual's talents are God-given; therefore, no one should be praised if he is an easy learner nor condemned if he is a slow learner. These differences in talent are God's will, and there is a place for each person God created. The teachers and children are tolerant of such differences. All children are expected to work hard and use their time well; they are not all expected to master the same amount of material. Their differences are not concealed, for though slowness in intellectual learning makes for added difficulties, it is nothing to be ashamed of. A motto displayed in one Amish school says,

> Little children you should seek
> Rather to be good than wise;
> For the thoughts you do not speak
> Shine out in your cheeks and eyes.

This attitude is not too different from that of the Hopi Indian: "A man need not be ashamed of being poor, or of being dumb, so long as he was good to others" (Lee 1959:20). A quick mind is not an asset in itself, but only when used properly. Many Amish believe that what is learned slowly is remembered better. Abraham Lincoln is quoted as saying, "My mind is like a piece of steel—very hard to scratch anything on it, but almost impossible after you get it there, to rub it out." Another motto expresses it this way:

> If you would have your learning stay,
> Be patient, don't learn too fast;
> The man who travels a mile each day
> May get around the world at last.

   Subject grades are given for achievement not effort. Daily and weekly grades are averaged mathematically with test grades to get the score that goes onto the report card. The children know what their daily grades are; in some schools they keep a record of their grades so they can also work out their own averages. A distribution curve that balances B's and D's and gives the majority of children C's is never used by the Amish. Not only are the number of pupils too small but this would lead to an unacceptable type of competition in which one child's good grade would depend on another child's poor grade. They prefer an absolute grading system in which a given number corresponds to a given letter grade. Grades are not manipulated to motivate the student; rather students are taught to accept the level of work they are able to do, to always work hard to do better, to "try, try again," and to remember that "it isn't so bad when you have tried and can't succeed as when you start thinking of giving up before you have really tried." Students are told, "God does not ask for success but for effort." Differences in ability are assessed realistically and accepted matter-of-factly. A mother will say, in front of her children, "This child is an easy learner," and pointing to another, comment, "He learns hard," in much the same way she might comment, "Reuben has blue eyes, Paul's are brown."

   Consistent with the oral tradition, Amish children commit a considerable amount of material to memory. They memorize poems the teacher selects and Bible verses. They memorize songs so they can sing while they work and will not be dependent on books. They sing and recite at their Christmas programs. All eight grades in one school that tested unusually high in arithmetic recited in unison the multiplication tables from 2 through 12 and the tables of conversions of measurements, weights, and volumes. The children enjoyed it as they would enjoy choral reading, and it never failed to impress visitors. It was a pleasant way for the children to

These children are doing their writing exercises at the blackboard (Photo by Vincent R. Tortora).

learn the arithmetic facts, for they did it as a group activity, protected from the embarrassment of obvious error by the carrying capacity of 40 voices. Just as the children memorize hymns and Bible verses before they really understand them, so these children knew their multiplication tables before they used or understood them.

The discussion method is not considered appropriate for academic subjects, for every child is expected to learn the facts and to be able to recite them. Instead of the children wildly waving hands and competing for the chance to answer, each child is questioned by the teacher, each is given his turn to answer, and each child answers the same number of questions. Learning is not disguised as a game. The children are taught that it is work, and although in the Amish culture work is something that must be done whether or not one likes it, whether or not it is convenient, the prevailing attitude is that people are fortunate to be able to work and that work is something to enjoy. "The spirit in happiness is not merely in doing what one likes to do, but to try to like what one has to do."

Discussion is used very effectively in areas where it applies. In many schools the children help to formulate the rules—although the teacher always has veto power—and these are openly and honestly discussed. Sometimes in the public schools the attempt to have a democratic classroom may blur the lines of decision making: the teacher "helps" the children democratically reach the "correct" decision (Jules Henry in Spindler 1963:230). This is not the case in Amish schools. If a decision is to be made by the teacher, the school board, or the parents, the decision is made without discussing it with the children and they are told what is acceptable.

When the children are invited to participate in a decision, however, their opinions are respected and they are actually allowed to reach their own decision. Because Amish schools are homogeneous and there is an emphasis on sensitivity to the group and on the individual's working for the good of the group, this effective procedure is good preparation for future participation in church decisions. The larger boundaries are set by the teacher as representative of the community; within these boundaries the children are given freedom of choice. So it will be for the adult church member.

Control is relaxed during recess and the noon hour when the children play vigorously, freely, and noisily. "Play at recess and noon opens our mind for study," said one teacher. Most schools have relatively few rules. The belief is that there should be few rules but these should be consistently enforced.

The Amish stress humility, the elimination of self-pride, mutual encouragement, persistence, the willingness to attempt a difficult task, and love for one another. A perusal of mottoes on schoolroom walls, of verses memorized, and of teachers' sayings illustrates the consistency of these values. For the Amish, education is primarily social rather than individual. Its goal is not "the freedom which exalts the individual" (Educational Policies Commission 1962:3), but social cohesion. Teaching the children to get along together in work and play is as important as teaching the academic subjects—both are essential for the continued existence of the Amish community. Specific teaching techniques and hints are mentioned in numerous teachers' letters and articles in the *Blackboard Bulletin*. The book *School Bells Ringing*, by Uria Byler, discusses methods for teaching every subject

Eighth-grade class at the blackboard (Photo by Vincent R. Tortora).

from phonics to health and also gives suggestions on such things as playing games, keeping the schoolhouse clean, and dealing with "newspaper pests." Over 80 teachers contributed to a book *Tips for Teachers, A Handbook for Amish Teachers* (Pathway Publishers 1970).

In the one- and two-teacher schools the number of pupils per teacher ranges from 13 to 47, with 27 as the average number. This number keeps the teachers busy. They have worked out a variety of ways for the children to help teach. In some schools the children exchange papers for checking. In other schools the older children help check the papers of the younger children. One teacher has the rule that grades five through eight may not read library books until the arithmetic papers for the lower grades have been corrected and that the third and fourth

Supervised reading, with an older pupil helping the younger ones (Photo by Vincent R. Tortora).

grades may not have library books until the first and second grade workbooks and arithmetic papers have been corrected. In other schools certain of the oldest children may help with reading words, give flash cards to the younger children, or listen to them read. Children also are permitted to help each other. These practices not only reinforce the children's learning by having them go over earlier material, but they also encourage concern and care for the younger children. Helping the teacher in specified ways is consistent with the Amish concept of sharing one another's burdens. However, the teacher must administer the program in such a way that she does not seem to the parents to shirk her leadership responsibility. Some teachers have a paid helper who answers hands. These are often girls who are recent graduates.

The Amish teacher is the recognized leader of the classroom, the one who is in charge and responsible. As would be expected, the Amish children identify closely with their teacher. Many of the mottoes and sayings used in the school include the teacher with the pupils:

> As the bird's song is refreshing every morning,
> so *we* should refresh each other with friendliness.

> Do *we* wonder at times what use *our* little life may be?
> Well, all that is asked from *us* is to fill *our* little
> place in this world as best *we* can.
> This could be a place important or one that is
> unimportant in the eyes of men.

Many of the teachers enjoy playing with the children during recess and the noon hour, as much as the children enjoy having them play. The school has the atmosphere of a well-ordered family, in which the teacher represents a parent or an older sibling. The pupils and teacher call one another by their first names, as is done throughout the Amish communities, where even the youngest children call the oldest women, the ministers, and the bishops by their first names. Respect is not based on titles.

The teachers plan occasional surprises for their pupils: a picnic in the woods, popcorn at noon, or a special trip. They may even plan a trip for their pupils during the summer. Sometimes a teacher will invite the children to her house for dinner, which is the noon meal. The children in turn have surprises for the teacher, especially for the teacher's birthday, when the children may hide a cake and lunch to surprise their teacher during the noon hour or after school. Often the teacher is a relative of many of the children and very likely attends the same church, so the children know their teacher in many roles, as a person in the community as well as in the classroom.

The children, under the teacher's direction, put on Thanksgiving and Christmas programs for the parents and invite them for a picnic on the schoolgrounds at the end of the term. The programs vary considerably from one community to another. In one school the children put on small skits, but this would be frowned on in other regions, where they sing religious songs and recite memory work. These programs provide a great deal of pleasure for the students, the parents, and the teachers. The children are beside themselves with excitement and delight as they enjoy one another's performance. One teacher said of their Thanksgiving program, "It was a heaping success."

Experienced Amish teachers are resourceful in maintaining their pupils' interest and in creating a pleasant school. The children and the teachers make school decorations. They may wash, dry, and crush eggshells which they then glue onto black paper to make mottoes. During the winter they make their own games. One class made "Farmopoly," a board game based on *Monopoly* but with dairy farms and harness shops instead of Boardwalk and public utilities. Sometimes a school will have a project of making a book. The children will each write an original story and then copy it into their own books. Some of the stories are illustrated. The excitement comes when everyone's book has been turned in and the stories are read aloud (without authors' names) to the class.

To summarize Amish methods of teaching, it may be said that Amish teachers

Lunchtime at a Pennsylvania school (Photo by Vincent R. Tortora).

are as much concerned with the development of Christian character, including a proper relational orientation to others, as with teaching facts. They are more concerned with giving their students correct knowledge than with teaching them critical thinking. The primary method used to instill correct knowledge is memorization and drill. Only within the framework of the material presented are the children taught to think for themselves. They are taught "what" and "where" but not "why" (except in theistic terms) and usually not "how" (except in a moral sense). In a secular school with a scientific orientation, children's analytic powers are trained to enable them to solve the "riddles of life, space, and time" (Educational Policies Commission 1961:9). In the Amish school these are not believed to be riddles that need to be solved by man. Truth need not be searched for, it has already been revealed (in the Bible), and it is there for those ready to believe. Because the Amish and the public schools have such different concepts of what truth is and how it is to be obtained, it is not surprising that their teaching methods are different: the Amish stress believing while the public schools stress questioning. Twentieth-century America not only should have room for both approaches, it needs both. Even the most rational questioner needs a basis in belief—though not necessarily a theological basis—from which to ask his questions and by which to judge his answers. And religious zeal needs the tempering of rational thought.

DISCIPLINE

Experienced Amish teachers from three states were asked, "What, in your opinion, constitutes good control in the schoolroom?" One teacher from Pennsylvania answered, "Good control is wearing a smile, regardless of how you feel inside. Be firm. Have a strong backbone, but not too stiff that it doesn't want to bend when necessary. A teacher should be humble." Another, from Ohio, said, "Be firm, not stern. . . . Have respect for the pupils, be honest with yourself and admit your mistakes if in the wrong. Be cheerful and slow to anger." Others mentioned trusting the children, not having too many rules, and being careful that no one, including the teacher, breaks them.

This same group of teachers was asked about the methods of discipline they used. The most common form was speaking to the offending child, often in private. Some teachers have the children apologize, but mention that "a false or forced apology is worse than none." A common punishment for a fairly serious offense is keeping children in their seats during recess or the noon hour. Sometimes, in addition, they have to write sentences during this period. Finally, corporal punishment, either a strap across the palm or paddling, may be used. Some teachers never use it; those who do state that it should be used very infrequently and with love. One teacher observed that it is "very effective but should be used with caution and plenty of love. I use it only for lying, cheating, vulgar language, or smutty talk, which is rare." Another teacher said, "We teachers should always see to it that punishing is done out of love. If it isn't, I believe it causes more harm than good, only causing rebellion on the part of the child." Physical punishment is used for the infractions mentioned above, for open disobedience, and for activity that is physically dangerous, such as children running into the highway or teasing a nervous buggy horse. Parents approve of limited use of physical punishment to enforce their children's moral and physical safety, but they do not tolerate physical punishment as a substitute for respect or as a means of frightening children into obedience. The occasional teacher who resorts to these methods soon finds himself looking for a different kind of employment.

Teachers use encouragement and rewards much more than punishment. Children are given stars, stickers, even pencils and candy bars for good behavior, good grades, and abiding by the rules. Not all teachers, however, approve of this. One teacher writes, "In my humble opinion, it works better to reward or treat the children unexpectedly, whether at home or at school, for their efforts and good work, *after* the task is done, rather than to promise rewards if they do this or that thing according to our wishes." Another teacher says she always has a treat for her pupils at the end of the six-weeks test day, not just for those who received 100 percent, but for each child who did his best. "Needless to say, no one admits not having done his best," one teacher said. Each one gets a candy bar, a pack of lifesavers, or some popcorn.

Amish teachers aim never to belittle their pupils or to use sarcasm or ridicule as a means of controlling them. They try to make the children understand their transgressions and accept punishment willingly—because it is deserved. Amish teachers feel emotionally very close to their pupils, and the children in turn admire and want to please their teachers.

TEACHER TRAINING

Most Amish teachers receive no formal training beyond eighth grade; however, new teachers use all available means for self-education. The Amish school system is in the process of becoming institutionalized and means are developing for the training and professional support of the teachers. In regions with a number of schools, teachers' meetings are held regularly.

A national Amish teachers' meeting is held annually, a teachers' publication (*The Blackboard Bulletin*) is issued monthly, and supplemental teaching material is being printed, including texts and teachers' manuals. Teachers also support one another by circle letters, visits to one another's schools, and frequent informal gatherings.

A national meeting of Amish teachers has been held annually since 1954. On the average, one-third of the teachers attend each year, in addition to board members, ministers, beginning teachers, and retired teachers. A teacher who has attended the first meeting and almost every one since wrote, "I believe these meetings have done more to create a better understanding of school matters than anything else." The two days are very full, but are pleasant and rewarding. Teachers from all states where the Amish live have an opportunity to meet one another and to talk informally as well as to listen to formal presentations on topics of practical interest.

The regional teachers' meetings function to bring teachers together for the opportunity of discussing their problems both formally and informally. They help the teachers realize that others have similar problems and successes. They function as training seminars in which the teachers learn how to handle their role. The teachers leave these meetings encouraged and anticipating ways they can improve their teaching and their schools.

The Amish teachers' journal, *Blackboard Bulletin,* founded in 1957, is an important publication serving the Amish school movement. It has a circulation of about 5,000. In keeping with the Amish tradition, its format is simple. Each year a list of schools is published. As the Amish schools become more institutionalized and the number of teachers increases, a limited professionalism is developing. Another publication, *Family Life,* issued by the same publisher, Pathway Publishing Corporation of Aylmer, Ontario, has appeared monthly since January, 1968. It is "dedicated to the promotion of Christian living among the plain people, with special emphasis on the appreciation of our heritage." Teachers read these periodicals for reinforcement of values, for news that affects them, for practical help in their classroom teaching, for help in their role as teacher, and for enjoyment of the stories and articles.

The contributors to the school journal are teachers, parents, and concerned Amish people, many of whom are widely read and value a good academic foundation. The editors have been careful to represent various Amish attitudes and have not been dogmatic in either their writings or their selections. The more conservative viewpoint is probably under-represented from the perspective of the total Old Order Amish culture. The most conservative individuals are not as motivated to write and are not as committed to an excellent school program. They still regard the school as a peripheral rather than an integral part of the community. Sensitive leadership and selfless hard work have produced a journal and a movement within the Amish culture that is meaningful to Amish people of the twentieth century.

Teacher training among the Amish continues to be primarily informal and personal. Some of the teachers work as helpers for a year or two before they take charge of a school. The apprentice system works well for the younger teachers, who serve full time under the direction of an experienced teacher. A helping teacher takes charge of the school for several days, which gives her an opportunity to learn how to manage a school while she still has the senior teacher available. Some of the teachers continue to take correspondence courses, although actual completion of high school is discouraged. The Amish feel that certain of the required courses are of no benefit to the Amish and that to work for a diploma is therefore a form of pride. The best preparation for teaching from the point of view of the Amish, in addition to the personal attributes of patience and a love of children and learning, is a firm grounding in the Amish faith. Informal means are used to train future teachers and to develop interest in teaching. Experienced teachers may talk to individual students who they think would make good teachers.

The informal support among Amish teachers constitutes a form of on-the-job teacher training. When they live near enough to one another, they may gather informally for supper and spend the evening with one another discussing school problems. The newer teachers visit the older teachers to ask about teaching methods and to learn such things as how to prepare a six-weeks test. Teachers compare parents and board members and problems and pleasures. They never meet without discussing aspects of school. Teachers may make friendship quilts for one another. Each teacher makes a square, the teacher whose quilt it is sets it up in a frame, and all the contributors gather for a quilting to finish the gift. Many teachers belong to one or more circle letters in which they discuss episodes and problems too personal or specific to be published in the teachers' journal.

Some professionalism is unavoidable, and in fact is desirable, even within this small, homogeneous subculture. As one Amishman put it, "It seems that after teaching school a while, a person gets a little hard to understand sometimes. And no wonder. Teaching is so far removed from farming or housekeeping that it takes just a little different kind of thinking, which is reflected in everyday living." Amish schools have a minimal bureaucracy that has no chance of growing into unworkable proportions. When the usual question is asked, "How can we improve our schools?," the answers are not those of the administrator or technician who thinks in terms of curriculum, buildings, or equipment. The Amish think in terms of character improvement, experience, knowing the pupils better, and bettering relations between teacher, pupils, parents, and board members.

RELATION TO PARENTS AND SCHOOL BOARD

There is some tension between the parents and the teacher. Teachers are sensitive to parental criticism and need their support. Because the teachers must be examples to the children as well as dispensers of information, they are especially vulnerable, for a teacher can be criticized not only for what or how she teaches, but how she dresses and spends her free time. The Amish believe very firmly that the training and conversion of children is the responsibility of the parents, not of the school—even an Amish school. The school teaches the child, and to that extent it is an extension of the parents, who have trained him well enough to make him receptive to the teaching he receives in school. The basis of classroom discipline is the respect of the children for the teacher and the teacher's respect for each child and each family. If the parents do not respect the teacher, the children feel this and the teacher soon has serious discipline problems.

The parents express their affection for the teacher in many ways. They bring her small gifts of food, they invite her to supper and to spend the night, and they may organize a birthday surprise for her. Sometimes the parents will get together and make a friendship quilt for her—perhaps with each child's signature embroidered on his family's square. In some of the schools the parents take turns bringing in a hot lunch once a month during the winter for the teacher and children. Unmarried teachers often try to spend at least one night a term in the home of every family in the school.

Parents are urged to visit their schools. Most schools leave it up to the parents' discretion when they should come, but their requests are persuasive. Parents are

Friendship quilt. Each square was made by an attending family and the completed quilt was given to the teacher (Photo by Charles S. Rice).

reminded that they don't put their steers out to pasture and never bother to check on them—and certainly their children are more valuable than cattle. Different schools have worked out various methods to get the parents to visit school regularly. In one school the parents drew dates out of a hat and then visited during their assigned week. In another school the parents decided to visit in order of the age of the father, with one couple coming each week. A teacher in Pennsylvania listed some of the advantages of parents' visiting school, and the disadvantages of their not visiting. Here are the advantages of regular parental visits:

1. Teacher gets an opportunity to visit with the parents.
2. Children get the feeling they (the parents) are a part of the school. It makes them feel important; they are being looked after.
3. The students have brushed up considerably in their lessons. They aren't going to be caught standing in class looking like a dumbbell.
4. Respect in many ways has greatly improved.
5. Teacher has the privilege to discuss discipline problems, if there are any, with the parents.

Here are the disadvantages if parents do not visit school:

1. Teacher has no fellowship with parents.
2. Children become careless; after all, no one is coming in to check on them except the teacher.
3. Children become rude.
4. Teacher has to work doubly hard to keep everyone happy and friendly.
5. Parents can not understand low report card marks.
6. Discipline problems are hard to overcome.

Many teachers feel that parental visits support the teachers' authority and make the job easier and more pleasant.

Parents come to the school when it is not in session to participate in frolics and work bees, to get the school and yard ready for the new term, to cut and stack wood, to repaint the woodwork, or to refinish the desks.

Many schools have meetings for the parents and board members every month. They strive for 100 percent attendance, but this is of course not possible. Teachers rely on these meetings. Any problems they have can be brought up then to get some idea of community consensus on what should be done; even if there are no problems, the meetings still serve a worthy function. These are evenings the teachers look forward to and delight in. One teacher says that the fathers trudging through the snow carrying their lanterns "show interest. And an evening together discussing farm sales, wood cutting, manure hauling, and school work is helping to lay a foundation for the future generation."

The teachers look to their school boards for guidance, support, and direction. The school board acts as a buffer between the teacher and the parents, between the teacher and the wider community, when such a buffer is needed. Most teachers say that they take all their problems to the school board. "My board is a great help by seeing that there are plenty of supplies, books, workbooks, especially for the lower grades, paper, pencils, etc. as needed. Last but not least important is their visiting the school frequently. It is encouraging when I meet the board members and they have smiles on their faces. I realize their job is not always the most pleasant, for they have the task of trying to satisfy the [Amish] taxpayers, parents, teachers and probably their wives and themselves," one teacher explained.

Any problems of noncooperation by parents or children are taken to the board. Good school board members consider their teacher's happiness. They stop on the way to town to inquire if she needs anything; they often have her over for supper and to spend the night; they may take her to church with them. Members of the school board often function as family for women or single men who are teaching outside their home church district. As is characteristic of the Amish culture, the relationship between the school board members and the school teacher is a personal one.

The school board hires and fires the teacher, woos her, and accepts her resignation. Many teachers seem to feel that it is not good to teach too long in the same school, and some parents believe that it is better if the children have more than one teacher during their years of schooling. A good teacher-board relationship was described by two teachers who said that, though this is their fourth year of teaching in the same school, they are treated as though it were their first. The school board and parents are anxious to have them stay. A problem may arise when a school board says nothing to a teacher about whether or not they want her back in the fall, since it is not the teacher's position to broach the subject unless she plans to leave. Experienced teachers recommend changing schools at least for one year if the teacher feels at all undecided about continuing.

School boards, in conjunction with parents, also make and implement decisions that affect the teachers' personal comforts—decisions to build a house for the teacher, set up a trailer for her, or build outside stairs at the home where she rooms so she can have her own entrance and not have to go through the family kitchen every time she leaves and enters. They must be concerned with all aspects of running the school, and therefore, with their teacher's equipment, living arrangements, and general contentment.

Uria R. Byler (1969) points out that it takes a lot of time and energy to be a good school board member and that those who serve should be "pushers," always working to keep the school going, to improve it, and to help start a new school when needed.

5 / The Amish vocational school

THE VOCATIONAL SCHOOL is the Amish response to state laws requiring children to spend more years in formal schooling beyond the eighth grade. Most states now require children to attend school until they are 16 or older. In some states children may apply for a farm work permit that excuses them from attendance at the age of 15. Legal problems arose in the past when local officials declined to issue farm permits and the Amish parents refused to send their children to consolidated high schools. Some children repeated the eighth grade one or more times until they were old enough to apply for a permit. After a number of years of conflict, from 1937 to 1955, the state of Pennsylvania permitted a compromise plan, worked out between the Pennsylvania Department of Public Instruction (Harrisburg, Pa., October 5, 1955) and the Amish leaders, called "Policy for Operation of Home and Farm Projects in Church-Organized Day Schools." According to this plan, pupils who have completed eighth grade but are not old enough to be eligible for a farm permit are to be enrolled in the vocational school. These schools, taught by an Amish person, are to offer "English, mathematics, health, and social studies, supplemented by home projects in agriculture and homemaking." Students are required to perform farm and household duties under parental guidance, keep a journal of their daily activities, and meet in classes a minimum of three hours per week. The Pennsylvania vocational plan has been adopted with modifications by the Amish elsewhere in the United States.

FORMAL ASPECTS OF THE VOCATIONAL SCHOOL

Typically the vocational class meets one afternoon a week. The following description of an Ohio school illustrates the schedule and the curriculum. The teacher in this school is an ordained minister who also helps draftees with their 1-W (conscientious objector status) assignments; however, conscientious objection is not discussed in the vocational school. About 30 children between the ages of 14 and 16 are in this school. (In Pennsylvania the children attend school only until their fifteenth birthday.) At one o'clock the teacher rings the bell and they sing in unison two or three songs, some German and some English. Then they stand and recite the Lord's Prayer in German. After this they copy their diaries, which they have been working on at home during the week, into their composition books, which are kept by the teacher. Meanwhile the teacher makes the attendance report. The ninth grade has arithmetic while the tenth grade works on English. The students use *Arithmetic in Agriculture* as their text. In English they learn such things as how to write a business letter. The classes change places and the tenth grade recites arithmetic while the ninth grade works on English. When the girls complained that too many of the problems had to do with planting fields and filling silos instead of figuring yard goods and modifying receipts, the teacher told them, "Some of you may marry men who are not so good with figures and you'll need to know how to help along with the figuring."

The children then have spelling. They have a spelling test on the words they were given the week before. This particular school uses *The New Stanford Speller: A Pupil-Activity Textbook*, which is also used in Indiana. Some teachers do all the grading; some allow the pupils to exchange papers for grading. Spelling grades are recorded each week. If there is time, the students may have a spelling bee in English. During the half-hour recess they play baseball if the weather permits. After recess the students read aloud in sequence from the German Testament. Because this teacher is a minister, he occasionally discusses the passages they read, but in most schools the New Testament is read without comment. This school is somewhat unusual in that each week the pupils are given a sheet of Bible questions which they take home to answer. They correct the answers during class the following week. Once a month they have a test on these questions. Occasionally they have a German spelling bee. The afternoon closes with the singing of three songs, both German and English, chosen and led, Amish style, by the children.

Learning to manage horses and produce crops is an important part of Amish vocational training (Photo by Vincent R. Tortora).

The vocational school teacher must keep a record of enrollment and attendance. Monthly reports are submitted to the school district office and to the county superintendent. Parents must supply written excuses for absences or tardiness. Report cards are sent to the parents monthly, rating the student on the following points: penmanship, reading, spelling, arithmetic, singing, German, homework, effort, behavior, whether he pays attention, whether he respects the teacher, whether he annoys others or whispers, whether the diary is satisfactory, times absent, and times tardy.

Teaching methods in the vocational schools vary with the age and background of the teacher. When the vocational school is taught by an elementary school teacher, she generally uses the same methods she uses with the younger children, including prizes such as candy bars or a quarter for correct memorization. The men teachers rarely give rewards for good grades or extra memorization. In one school each pupil has his own notebook. Every week they trade books and write a memorized German Bible verse into a friend's book, sign the verse, and read it aloud. "By the end of the term, we have all written in each other's notebooks a number of times. This is something to keep and read and also to compare writing," it was explained. Vocational school pupils generally enjoy their classes.

A SCHOOL WITHOUT WALLS

The major portion of the curriculum is the home projects in agriculture and homemaking, which require doing rather than all-day book learning. A week's excerpts from the diary of a boy and a girl in Lancaster County, Pennsylvania, indicate the varied skills these 14-year-olds are mastering.

From Chester's Diary

Mon.	Checked the meadow fence for [electrical] shorts. Shovel-harrowed garden and concreted chicken house.
Tues.	Chopped wood and cleaned boards.
Wed.	Made a new door for the cow stable in the afternoon.
Thurs.	Went to school in the forenoon. Filled silo in the afternoon.
Fri.	Filled silo in forenoon. Watched cows in the afternoon.
Sat.	Washing cow stable in forenoon. Fixing an engine on the corn sheller and shelling corn in P.M.
Sun.	Stayed at home. Had company afternoon.

From Rebecca's Diary

Mon.	I helped with the Mon. work [washing and ironing] and daily chores.
Tues.	I was mending in the A.M. and unloading wood in the P.M. and culling chickens in the eve.
Wed.	Sewed in the A.M., washed eggs in the P.M.
Thurs.	Made a new door for the cow stable in the afternoon.
Fri.	I helped butcher a hog.
Sat.	I took down tobacco most of the day, and cleaned the upstairs.

On different days Chester describes fixing various engines and machines that break down; digging up and cleaning piping; rebuilding a kitchen; rebuilding the chicken house; cementing and building a cow pen; butchering; plowing, disking, harrowing, and rolling the various fields; cleaning the barn; hauling manure; helping with the washing; and innumerable other tasks essential to successful farm management. Rebecca describes mowing and trimming the yard, picking up potatoes, working in the garden, husking corn, taking care of neighbors' children, raking the barnyard, refinishing furniture, baking, canning pears and applesauce, helping the men cement the cow stables, painting the kitchen, crocheting, and stripping tobacco. She is learning the various tasks useful to a farmer's wife. Not only do the children learn how to do the actual tasks required, but they also learn how to help with one another's work. Although most jobs are executed primarily by men or by women, they help one another with extra work. Thus, Rebecca helped the men with the cementing and Chester helped "mom" with the washing. The children also learn the pattern of activity. "I helped with the Monday work. . . . I did the Friday work in the morning. . . . I finished the Saturday work." They learn to help the neighbors and the extended family. "Today I was taking care of Amos King's, Jacob Fisher's, and Jonathan Stolzfus' children." "Did neighbor's work. . . . Worked for Grandfather. . . . Hauled church benches."

These young people are learning not only how to do the necessary work but also when to do it, how to incorporate each task with other necessary activities, and how work functions both within their family and within the wider community. They learn to enjoy the work and to see it as creative, both in the immediate results and in its contribution to the comfort and happiness of others. This attitude toward manual work is a contrast to that taught, for example, in home economics courses in public high schools, where "in itself, it [work] contains no good" (Lee: 1963:183). In American high schools manual work is associated with efficiency but not with satisfaction. The Amish obtain greater emotional satisfaction from manual labor than do most public school graduates.

Although many of the Amish communities base their vocational schools on the Pennsylvania plan, there are some adaptations. The Indiana agreement (Wells 1967) is more limiting in its description of the vocational project, for the state school officials were apparently thinking in terms of 4-H projects rather than learning a life vocation. One of the Amish signees pointed out:

> Here is where I feel he [the state superintendent of education] does not understand our faith. . . . In our vocational setup he requires a project similar to a 4-H project. . . . What we want is that children can help along with the necessary work, and thereby learn their life vocation by doing. But to the public this looks too much as if we want them at home to help do our work, which we can not deny in many cases, for this all fits in with our way of life and our faith. They are helping do the family work, under the care and discipline of the parents, and are learning something more useful than all-day book learning.

Project areas specified by the Indiana agreement include livestock and poultry, fruits and vegetables, grains, tools and equipment, building construction and maintenance, farm finances and management, carpentry, landscaping and horti-

Amish boy hoeing in the field (Photo by Vincent R. Tortora).

culture, homemaking, and gardening. Daily chores and other routine household duties do not count as part of a vocational project, except where they are a necessary part of a project. Projects must be supervised by the vocational teacher. Services outside the home may be included as projects only when done in cooperation with neighbors and by consent of parents and the instructor.

Some school officials still scoff at the Amish vocational school. One county superintendent of schools said, "These three-hour schools are mostly a waste of time." The Amish are grateful for the vocational plan. Aaron Beiler, long-time chairman of the Amish Church School Committee (from 1937 to 1968), said: "We Amish feel obliged for the reasonable attitude in Pennsylvania. We know that when our children are brought up our way, they are satisfied with our way of life. If they go into the higher grades they will become dissatisfied." Many of the adults who attended vocational school speak highly of their experience in the school. One girl had this to say: "I am not sorry for all the German songs and verses I learned in vocational school. . . . As I go about my work I can sing many songs that I learned in school. It is a pastime to sing while you work, and it makes work seem like play just to have songs in your thoughts."

Through the vocational plan the Amish have been able to combine the teaching of technical skills and the job role. Techniques can be taught within the four walls of the school, but competence in work can be acquired only by doing. There is a job etiquette that must be learned, and the best way to learn it is outside of the school, working at a real job in a protected and directed manner. This is managed admirably by having the children work under the direction and supervision of the parents. The young men learn not only how to perform a task, such as how to harrow, but also when to harrow, and how to integrate harrowing into all the other work associated with farming. The young Amishmen learn how to interact with other people in work relationships. While they are learning techniques, they are also learning a job role. Apprentice experience enables the young person to develop a realistic concept of what he will be doing as an adult. This type of schooling is related to life and comes close to the Amish definition of an educated person: a "man is educated who is on to his job" (Beiler 1961:6).

The Amish vocational school is truly a school without walls. In school pupils are taught by a teacher and in their work projects they are under the supervision of parents and adults. Such education has formality and structure even though it is

Young children learn to work together in doing farm chores (Photo by Vincent R. Tortora).

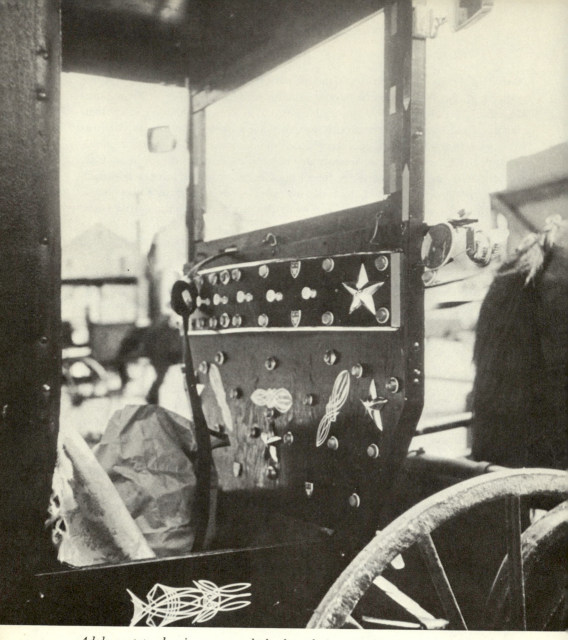

Adolescent tendencies to exceed the boundaries may be seen on this buggy, with its many rear-view mirrors, light switches, and decorations (A Fred Wilson Photo).

not all carried out in a specific building. The natural authority of the parents and the needs of the children are brought together in a way that is positive for the growth of the culture. On the whole, the children view the adults as protectors and as models in the process of assuming adult responsibility.

THE AMISH "DROPOUT"

What happens to the Amish child who does not wish to terminate his education with the Amish system? The answer is very simple. Any child who continues his schooling into high school, either immediately after completing the eighth grade or later, will not remain Amish. It is extremely rare for a child who has attended Amish schools to enter high school. This may occur if his family changes church affiliations by joining a liberalized group. Occasionally a few Amish pursue higher education in their late teens or after the age of 21 by taking correspondence courses or by attending a Mennonite institution. The number of such persons is decidedly limited but appears to be on the increase. Such persons usually choose to become nurses or teachers, professions that are least objectionable and that will be useful to the more liberalized segments of the Amish community. An insatiable desire for learning is manifest in a few.

Amish persons who pursue higher education usually come from families who themselves are liberal or atypical in some way. The parents may be lenient in respect to the rules of the community, or perhaps one of them has secretly nursed the aspiration to follow a profession outside of the Amish pattern, as a teacher, businessman, or missionary, for example. Such unfulfilled aspirations of parents may be sensed by the young and taken as their own life goals. If families are both large and somewhat marginal to the Amish discipline, the young are less likely to find meaningful work satisfaction on the family farm.

By typical American standards the Amish children are all dropouts, for they do not enter high school. But from the Amish point of view, the Amish child who continues his training through high school and college is a dropout from the Amish religion and way of life. Lack of formal training, however, is no problem for the Amish in obtaining employment in the community. In most settlements where the Amish live, their skills as maids, baby-sitters, housecleaners, laborers, farm tenants, carpenters, builders, and factory workers are sought by the non-Amish people. Many small industries would rather hire Amish persons with only an elementary education than high school graduates, who they say are less likely to be dependable and prompt and are less inclined to give a full day's work. The Amish will not work in unionized plants, however.

There is little foundation to the notion advanced by some that the Amish should be forced to take more years of schooling so that in case they should leave the faith, they would not be disadvantaged educationally. Individuals of Amish background who decide to obtain a higher education are generally highly motivated and capable of doing so. As in any minority group some Amish individuals have personal problems due to culture change and conflict, but these persons do not become a burden on society or welfare recipients.

Young people of the more liberalized affiliations of Amish, who have adopted modern technology and travel but who have limited sophistication for coping with the problems these innovations can entail, may feel a greater degree of stress and uncertainty than the Old Order youth. We have not included such groups in the scope of this study. The Old Order Amish children genuinely aspire to do the things their parents are doing. They are not impoverished by their own social institutions, nor are they denied emotional or actual participation in their society.

6 / Personality

and achievement patterns

PERSONALITY TYPE

THE HABIT SYSTEMS of a large number of individuals in a society can be studied in order to discover the type of personality most manifest in the society, sometimes called the modal personality. Benedict's study (1957) of the Pueblos, for example, reported a basic set of personality traits for the society as a whole: "sobriety, moderation, orderliness, and cooperativeness." By such a study of the Amish—in spite of many difficulties, including that of devising tests for cross-cultural comparison—we hoped to discover the extent of homogeneity or heterogeneity in Amish personality and the basic personality type. Despite the methodological problems, we found evidence that Amish personalities are shaped by their social milieu, that Amish child-training and educational practices as described in earlier chapters correspond with a "psychic unity" among the Amish. The evidence we found for an Amish type is based on the results of the Myers-Briggs personality indicator, an examination of children's drawings, and an analysis of vocational preferences.

Myers-Briggs Type Indicator. (By Isabell Briggs Myers, Educational Testing Service, Princeton, New Jersey, 1962.) This test is designed to ascertain a person's basic preference pattern in regard to perception and judgment. A person may reasonably be expected to develop most skill with the processes he prefers to use and in the areas of his interests. The items in the test offer forced choices between given alternatives. A typical question might be: "Would you rather work under someone who is (a) always kind or (b) always fair?" A person's personality type is determined by a letter combination of 16 possible types derived from 4 basic indexes:

EI   Extraversion or Introversion
SN   Sensing or Intuition
TF   Thinking or Feeling
JP   Judgment or Perception

The scores are computed so that an individual has either E or I, S or N, T or F, J or P. An individual's type is expressed in a four-letter combination such as ENTP. The EI index is designed to reflect whether the person is predominantly an extravert or an introvert, whether he is oriented to the world of people and things or to the inner world of concepts and ideas. The SN index is designed to reflect the person's preferences between two opposite ways of perceiving, sensing and intuition. The TF index reflects the individual's preferences between two opposite ways of judging—thinking or logical processes versus feeling or subjective processes. The JP index is designed to reflect whether the individual relies primarily on a judgment process (coming to a conclusion) or a perceptive process (awareness).

The most dominant type to emerge among the 251 Amish children in our sample was ISFJ. Almost 30 per cent of the Amish were of this type, as compared to only 6.4 per cent of the non-Amish in our sample, and 24 per cent of the Amish were ESFJ. This degree of homogeneity of personality type is unique to the Amish, differing from national samples and from all other non-Amish children we tested. (For supporting tables and data, see the research report: Hostetler 1969: 225–232.) Whether in their own schools or in public school, the Amish showed the same pronounced type. The test manual (Myers 1962:70) gives this description of the ISFJ type:

> Quiet, friendly, responsible and conscientious. Works devotedly to meet his obligations and serve his friends and school. Thorough and painstaking, accurate with figures but needs time to master technical subjects, as reasoning is not his strong point. Patient with detail and routine. Loyal, considerate, concerned with how other people feel even when they are in the wrong.

This characterization matches our observations of the Amish. Perhaps no observational data could yield a description of Amish personality characteristics more appropriate than this one. According to the results, the Amish personality configurations are least like those of science students and research scientists. The Amish have a very high percentage of Sensing-Feeling preferences, approaching those of sales and customer relations employees (Myers 1962:Table D5). The test predicts that the Amish personality type will find most satisfaction in occupations requiring dependability, tact, sympathy, hard work, and a systematic approach to work. The type harmonizes with Amish cultural themes and values stressed in their society. There was little difference between the response patterns of Amish girls and boys.

The *introvert* likes quietness and concentration in preference to variety and distraction, tends to be careful with detail, prefers not to work fast with complicated procedures, and does not mind working on one project for a long time without interruption. These tendencies contrast with those of the *extravert*, who tends to be impatient with long, slow jobs and is interested in the idea behind the job rather than in how other people do the job. The introvert works well alone and tends to dislike generalities.

The *sensing* type dislikes new problems unless they can be solved in standard ways. He prefers an established routine, enjoys using skills he has already acquired, and works more steadily than the *intuitive* type, who may work in bursts of energy powered with enthusiasm. He becomes impatient when the details are too complicated to remember. He seldom makes errors of fact and tends to be good at precise work.

The *feeling* type tends to be very aware of other people and of feelings and likes to please people or help them, whereas the *thinking* type may hurt people's feelings

In my
happy time
I like to bake

"My happy time" drawing by girl age 15.

without knowing it. He likes harmony in contrast to analysis, and his efficiency may be badly disturbed by feuds. He dislikes telling people unpleasant things; he finds it difficult to reprimand people or to fire them even when necessary. He is sympathetic, needs people around him, and relates well to most people.

The *judging* type likes to plan his work and finish it on schedule rather than adapting to changing situations. He does not have trouble making decisions but may decide things too quickly. Unlike the *perceptive* type, who likes to work rapidly with complicated tasks, he does not like to start many projects at the same time. He may tend to overlook new things that need to be done. He tends to be satisfied with a judgment on a thing, situation, or person once it is reached.

It will be recognized that many of these characteristics correspond to the values stressed in Amish culture. Respect for others, consideration, helpfulness, sympathy, and even pacifism correspond with the strong *feeling* component of the test, particularly the notion of being "concerned with how other people feel even when they are in the wrong." Such personality endowments help explain why the Amish can be so steady in their work and so steadfast in their faith and how they can adhere so faithfully to the *Ordnung.* These preferences and personality patterns, which the Amish learn as children, remain with them as they become adults.

Freehand drawings Children were instructed to draw "Your house—the house in which you live" and "My happy time—what you do that you most enjoy." (The instructions were written by Dale B. Harris and appear in the research report:

Hostetler 1969:341–343.) Children's drawings reveal many aspects of personality, especially how the child views his environment and himself. The drawings of Amish and non-Amish were compared to ascertain whether their themes varied and whether their content was consistent with the value orientations of the children's respective cultures.

Happy-time drawings The two cultures exhibited some striking differences. The Amish happy-time drawings include work-related activities, whereas the non-Amish drawings contained not a single work-related drawing. Amish work-related activity included such tasks as baby-sitting, raking leaves, gathering eggs, and baking. These activities are obviously important in the lives of the Amish children, for they perform such duties as part of the routine of living on the farm. Non-Amish children are probably given fewer assigned tasks and their participation in work is less important to the functioning of the household than in the Amish home. Certainly such tasks are not associated with happiness. Other Amish happy-time drawings depicted reading, eating, sledding, fishing, ice-skating, playing ball, swinging, hunting, and going on a trip.

The non-Amish happy-time drawings showed marked competitive activity and some hostility. They included swimming, snowball fights, hitting the teacher with a snowball, throwing an object at an automobile, playing basketball, buying new things at the store, wrestling with the dog, and "blowing up the school."

The Amish included others in their drawings to a much greater extent than did the non-Amish. Being with others is apparently important to Amish children, and when they draw pictures of a happy time, they see themselves as part of a group. Their drawings appear less individualistic than the non-Amish drawings.

Amish children more frequently than the non-Amish included outdoor activity in their drawings. Amish boys showed a greater preference for outdoor activity than did Amish girls, which is consistent with Amish adult roles. Non-Amish children do not aspire to be farmers or to work outdoors and their drawings show more indoor activity than the Amish drawings. The Amish boys depicted activities somewhat different from those depicted by Amish girls, but these differences were not as great as between the non-Amish boys and girls. Amish male activities are related to the adult male role in the farm environment, but many Amish girls also prefer such male-related activities as fishing or working with animals. The absence of a strong differentiation of activities between the sexes suggests that, at least for elementary school age, the Amish have no rigid dichotomy between male and female concepts of "a happy time."

House drawings Amish drawings include large farmhouses, often with a variety of color and many windows, and other features of the farm environment— such as porches on the house, walks, gardens, roads, and even mudholes. The drawings reflect regional aspects of Amish culture, so that those of us who knew the several communities could tell from the style of the architecture or landscape in the drawing whether the drawing came from a community in Ohio, Indiana, or Pennsylvania.

The children were instructed to "write something about your house if you wish." Amish children wrote comments such as: "This is the house where I live,"

My Happy Time
Off for another galloping ride.
"Get up."

"My happy time" drawing by boy age 15.

"I like my home," "I like to work in my house and barn." They had positive feelings about their homes. Many of their drawings included other dwellings or objects— a barn, sidewalks, or a garden—which they thought of as part of the home. In contrast the non-Amish rarely drew surrounding buildings and sometimes drew only their own bedroom or a single room in the dwelling. Amish children learn that "home is not a place to go when there is no other place to be, but the center of all good things." The Amish children's use of color differed greatly from one school to another. They used green and blue, but they also made liberal use of red, yellow, and brown.

Regulation and conformity, rather than spontaneity, are dominant characteristics in their drawings, as was also observed in fieldwork. The drawings indicate that

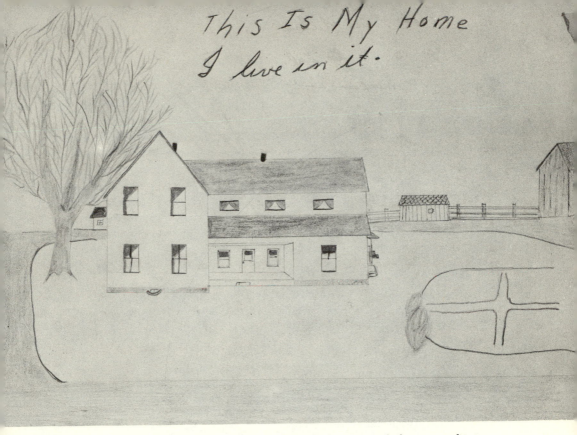

"My home" drawing by girl age 15. The concept of home includes more than a house.

rule is important in the life of both Amish boys and girls. These drawings show some of the dominant Amish personality characteristics, interests, self-conceptions, and patterns of interaction with the environment. The Amish children depict their external environment at an unusually early age. They use color realistically from the age of six. They are able to make spatial relationships at an early age, an important indication of social growth and socialization. The deemphasis of the self and the importance of the group (family and community) show that the Amish child is responding at a very young age to the external environment and the value patterns of Amish culture, which emphasize the family and the church-community, not the individual. External rather than subjective elements seem dominant in the drawings.

Vocational preferences Personality characteristics are revealed by attitudes toward work and by vocational interests. Amish children were asked to write a short theme on the topic, "what kind of work I want to do when I grow up, and why," and to give their age, sex, and the occupations of their fathers. This method of investigation, used by Goodman (1957) and by Freed and Freed (1968), reveals not only vocational aspirations, but also the extent of continuity of interests between the old and the young.

Responses were obtained from Amish and non-Amish groups of children. The Amish children were from both traditional communities in densely populated settlements and from communities that were relaxed with respect to the older traditions. Some of the less traditional schools were in small settlements or were geographically marginal to the larger communities. The 242 Amish responses were grouped into "traditional" and "nontraditional" Amish vocations and the vocational preferences were compared to the actual occupations of the household heads.

The pupils in the traditional communities generally chose vocations in keeping with the Amish values. They were farm-related and included trades associated with the Amish way of life: carpentry, harness-making, blacksmithing, working in a carriage repair shop, sawmilling, logging, woodworking, and often a choice of farming combined with another occupation. A few responses representative of those that followed the traditional vocational pattern are these:

An Amish boy, 9 years old, wrote:

> When I grow up I want to be a good farmer. Because I like to milk and feed the pigs, chickens, horses, cows, and calves. Also I get the straw and hay down. . . . Father teaches me to farm.

An Amish boy, 13 years old and in the eighth grade, wrote:

> I want to be a farmer and this is why. I like farming because I like to get up early in the morning and do the chores. When I have eaten I like to go out in the fields and plow or disk or whatever needs to be done. When I need a tool shed to put my tools in, I would build a building because I like to hammer nails. When I would break something I would go to town and buy a new part, or if I had a welder I would weld it. When it is time to make hay I would try to get my neighbors to help and would bring the hay in after dark when it is nice and cool.

A girl, age 13, wrote:

> When I grow up I want to be a housekeeper, bake, cook, iron, wash, and have a garden. I don't want to live in the city. I would have a few flower beds in the lawn so it wouldn't look so bare. I want to be a housekeeper, because my mother taught me how to cook. I want to have a garden so I wouldn't have to buy the vegetables and things. I don't want to live in the city so that I wouldn't have to hear all the noise. I want to work out, to help people.

An Amish girl in her last year of elementary school explains what she hopes to do when she becomes an adult:

> I would want to live on a farm and keep house. I would want to bake, sew, cook, wash clothes, iron, make Christmas candy to sell, knit mufflers, and many other things. I would want a lawn to mow, trim, and rake. I would have very nice flowers all around the house. I would bake bread and rolls. I'd make pattys and doughnuts ever so good. I'd make noodles too.
>
> I would live on a farm too so I'd always have lots of work. I'd help milk cows, feed a dog, a dozen cats and kittens and the chickens, too, so I don't have to buy eggs. I'd help in the fields and put hay in. I would help other neighbors too with their work, so when I need help they'll help me too. I would spend a day at my parents, brothers, or sisters places too. I think I'd find time to visit at Sam Yoder's school one afternoon.
>
> The reason why I'd want to live on a farm and keep house is because there are always so many interesting things to do which I enjoy.

These children look forward with happy anticipation to the roles they will fill as adults.

Those occupational choices that ordinarily can not be carried out on the family farm were grouped as nontraditional. They included working in a restaurant, working in a factory, nursing, teaching, being an editor, managing a bookstore, and being a cowboy. The vocation of teacher is difficult to classify, since this role is emerging as an acceptable one in Amish society. It is presently regarded as a calling rather than a form of making a living. The following responses are representative of nontraditional vocations:

A boy, age 8, wrote:

> When I grow up I would like to be a fire chief of a town whose population would be about 8,000. I would want to drive a big firetruck. The reason I want to be a fire chief is because I could give orders. I also like to go to fires, or maybe I could rescue somebody.

A boy, age 13, wrote:

> I would like to be a man that handles books a lot. A librarian, a secretary, or anything that has to do with books. I like almost any kind of books but I prefer westerns and mystery books. Since my mother was also a bookworm I guess I got the love of books from her. Anyway in my spare time I want a book in my hands.

A boy in grade 2, age 7, wrote:

> I want to be an auctioneer. I like to shout.

A girl in her last year of elementary school, age 13, wrote:

> When I grow up I want to be a waitress in a restaurant. I have always wanted to wait on people. But I have never thought of being a waitress till lately. I would like to work six days a week, Monday till Saturday. I think it would be fun to wait on people, because then I would meet other people. But I would want to come home every evening.

Such responses came from Amish schools that were marginal with respect to traditional Amish customs. Yet each of the nontraditional vocational choices was a service occupation and each reflected parental preferences and love of work. It would appear that even when Amish children choose marginal occupations, the general value pattern of the culture is maintained. The choices are consistent with rather than antagonistic to the Amish value orientation.

In a public school with a student population composed of approximately one-third Amish and two-thirds non-Amish, the Amish children responded very differently from their non-Amish schoolmates. The dominant choice of the Amish boys was farming, with many specifying dairy farming, hog raising, horse farming, or simply, "I wish to be a farmer." In one school where there were 28 Amish boys, 18 wished to be farmers. Of 38 non-Amish boys in the same school, only 3 chose farming as an occupation. Other non-Amish choices fell into the professional category: scientists, government service, astronaut, artist, and leader in sports. Amish girls in public school showed a marked preference for service-oriented vocations, such as teaching and nursing. Their other choices were in the category of unskilled manual labor, such as housekeeping: "be a housewife," "work at somebody else's house," "cleaning house, taking care of the children, and cooking." The non-Amish girls preferred such vocations as secretary, actress, modeling; none preferred a vocation that could be classed as unskilled manual labor.

Clearly Amish children have a concept of value pattern for vocation different from that of non-Amish children. They see and are taught that their fathers hold their jobs because of an "Amish way of life." They emulate the occupations of their fathers and mothers and sense no stigma attached to aspiring toward such a role. They know through participation in adult activities that they can fulfill their aspirations when they become adults. The children in the Old Order Amish community know what they want to do; they know what they will be doing when they become adults; and they are receiving the emotional, psychological, and technical training essential for productive adulthood as Amish men and women.

ACHIEVEMENT PATTERNS

We wanted to understand Amish achievement patterns not only in relation to non-Amish children in American society, but also in relation to Amish cultural goals. We needed to find a group of tests that would be appropriate and reliable, to obtain the cooperation of the Amish schools, and to test a sufficient number of children. These problems are discussed in greater detail in the research report (Hostetler 1969:43–54) and in a dissertation by Wayne Miller (1969), who assisted in the research. Especially important for our purposes was a knowledge of the Amish school setting, the function and nature of testing in their schools, and their attitude toward standardized tests.

Amish testing practices Amish teachers give periodic tests in the basic subjects they teach. Speed, however, is not stressed in Amish schools. Children are admonished to do careful, accurate work. It is considered better to do what one does well, rather than to do a great deal and make careless mistakes. The pupils are taught not to skip material they do not understand, but to work at it until they have mastered it. The Amish always give their own tests without time limits, for they do not want the children to hurry. Amish children who attend public school often complain, "They never let me finish anything." The Amish child in such a setting works under a heavy disadvantage, since he loses his sense of continuity, expression, and personal fulfillment. This difference in time orientation places Amish children at a disadvantage when taking standardized tests. Instead of learning to work quickly, guess intelligently, and skip those questions they do not understand, the Amish children are taught: "Do not rush over your work in school or at home." "Take your time when making important decisions." "People who are always in a hurry, seemingly, get very little satisfaction out of life." The children are cautioned not to be "like the world," but to "be contented, and do not worry or try to follow up the world's uneasiness and speed." "Look up into the branches of the trees, knowing that they grew great and strong because they grew slowly and well."

Some Amish schools give achievement tests, but they are very different from most standardized tests. These tests, made up by the Amish teachers, are given usually at the end of six-weeks marking periods. At the termination of the school year in some Amish communities, eighth-grade pupils are given a special examination. In one region in Ohio the test is given in two sections, the first section at the pupils' own school, the second section at a larger gathering—where the teachers take this test too. At their own school the pupils write the counties of Ohio in alphabetical order and the names of the presidents of the United States in order of election; they draw freehand a map of their county, filling in each township, and they label an outline map of the United States with the states and capitals. All eighth graders from about a dozen schools gather at the conclusion of the school year for the second section of the achievement test. This test is made up by the teachers, who send in 10 questions on each subject to one of the former teachers. Four or five former teachers get together and select 20 arithmetic problems, 10 English questions, 10 American geography questions, 20 spelling words, 5 questions on Canadian geography, 5 on Latin American geography, and 10 on Ohio history. The two-room schools in this settlement are built with a movable partition "so we can put it up for the eighth-grade tests." This community-wide effort of making and administering the test has proven to be popular among the teachers, pupils, and families.

Amish cultural factors and use of standardized tests   The Amish children in our study were not practiced in taking standardized tests. Standardized tests are designed by people who have a very different philosophy of education and different ideas of what is general information for young children than do the Amish. We were also aware of differences in motivation between the Amish and non-Amish children. Amish pupils, for example, see no purpose in formal schooling beyond the elementary grades, and doing well on a standardized test offers no incentive for a better-paying job or entrance into high school. We wondered whether the Amish children would spend too much time on single questions, for they had never been coached in taking standardized tests. We wondered if Amish children (like lower-class children) would be less verbal, more fearful of strangers, less self-confident, and less motivated toward scholastic achievement than middle-class children. We took the position that we were working with healthy children, and we chose proven rather than experimental tests or those that measure pathological tendencies. Our approach to the research was not that the children were having social problems.

Pretesting helped us locate items in the tests that the Amish did not understand, that did not apply to them, or that were taboo. The pretesting convinced us that it took too long to administer all the tests we wanted. The intrusion of a two-day testing program was too strenuous, so we reduced the program to two half-days.

Amish attitudes toward testing, we found, vary among schools and communities. Some schools permitted testing but did not wish to have the children draw the human figure in the draw-a-man test. Their objection was part of the general taboo against photography and representation of the human figure. Attitudes toward testing also varied with the experience and training of the teacher. The most interest in standardized testing generally was shown by those teachers who had taught for a long time and who were secure in their role in relation to their school board and their community. But some still felt that, in the long run, testing may be harmful to the Amish, even if it is done by sympathetic outsiders.

Only after investing large amounts of time with school board members and teachers was it possible to obtain the cooperation of a sufficient number of schools. It was necessary for our staff to go over the tests themselves, often item by item, with school board members. In one community two years elapsed between the time the tests were explained and the time when consent was obtained. Most parents were not interested in knowing their children's achievement scores and did not think that comparing them to scores of other children in the United States was important. The notion that the usefulness of the individual is related to a test score is foreign to the Amish, for they believe that each individual has a God-given role in this world. They firmly reject channeling individuals into those vocations that are considered useful to a complex technological society (Friedenberg 1970). They reject occupations in science, industry, the military, and government.

The research design The design for testing achievement patterns took into account academic subjects that were important to Amish cultural goals. We were interested in assessing educational goals in the context of intercultural relations. Our interest was in subjects the Amish mastered well. There were many school officials who doubted whether the Amish were capable of running their own schools. They were skeptical of the achievement of children who attended schools in which teachers were not certified and in fact had not attended college.

The schools we included in the study had in most cases been in existence for two or more years. The teachers were experienced, having taught no less than three years; they were considered by the community to be good teachers. In addition to testing the pupils in these schools, we also observed many other schools in different communities. Since reading, writing, and arithmetic are important in Amish educational goals, we chose tests for these areas, covering vocabulary, reading comprehension, spelling, English grammatical word usage, and ability to solve practical problems. Most Amish schools have limited library facilities. We were interested in how this affected the ability to use reference material, and we gave a test in this area. We also gave a standardized test in the use of sound reasoning technique and one on general intelligence. In addition we gave the pupils a nonverbal test of intelligence.

Our aim was to compare Amish schoolchildren objectively with children who attended public schools. We compared Amish schools having noncertified teachers with public schools having certified teachers, and consolidated schools with Amish country-schools having all eight grades. Because of their limited access to mass media and because of the use of English as a second language, we anticipated incorrectly that the Amish would score lower than the non-Amish children in public school. We were surprised.

The achievement tests were given to grades 5, 6, 7, and 8. In our study, however, we focused special attention on the achievement of the eighth grade; this is the point at which Amish children have had the maximum exposure to formal education. We were interested in comparing Amish and non-Amish achievement scores at the completion of the eighth grade. We were also interested in discovering whether the achievement scores were different in integrated schools, where Amish and non-Amish attended the same school. We therefore chose representative groups of eighth-grade pupils, 25 or more, in each of the following social settings:

1. Amish in public schools where all pupils who attended were Amish.
2. Amish in privately operated or parochial Old Order Amish schools.
3. Amish in public schools where Amish and non-Amish attended in about equal proportions.
4. Rural non-Amish who attended public school with the Amish in about equal proportion.
5. Rural public schools with no Amish.

The control groups consisted of pupils in a modern rural school system, selected and matched for their general economic proximity to that of the Amish. The several tests and the results are given below.

STANDARDIZED TEST RESULTS

SRA Tests of Educational Ability (Technical Supplement for Grades 4–6 and 9–12; Third Edition, 1963.) The average composite score for language, reasoning, and quantitative ability for the eighth-grade Amish was 96.7 and for the non-Amish, 99.5, a difference that was not statistically significant (see Table 1). The scores showed no significant difference between the Amish in their own schools, those in all-Amish public schools, or those in public schools with non-Amish pupils (Hostetler 1969:167).

The Amish children scored significantly lower ($P < .01$) in the language section of the IQ test than did the control group. Although the Amish pupils scored higher than the non-Amish in the sections on reasoning and quantitative ability (Table 1), the difference was not significant.

Iowa Tests of Basic Skills (E. F. Lindquist and A. A. Hieronymus. Boston, Massachusetts: Houghton Mifflin Co. 1964.) Six of the eleven possible testing areas were administered: vocabulary, reading comprehension, spelling, word usage, knowledge and use of reference materials, and arithmetic problem solving. When scores of the Amish and the control groups were compared by subject matter, the Amish excelled in spelling, word usage, and arithmetic (see Table 2). These differences are statistically significant in favor of the Amish.

The non-Amish control group overtook the Amish in vocabulary. In use of reference material and reading comprehension the two groups were virtually equal. In other words, only in [English] vocabulary did the non-Amish children outperform the Amish children. There were no significant differences in the Iowa achievement scores between the Amish in public schools and those in Amish schools except in the area of word usage. The students in Amish schools did significantly better in word usage than did the Amish students in public schools (Miller 1969:132, 153). The composite achievement scores for all skills tested ranked by group from high to low in this order: Amish pupils in Amish schools,

TABLE 1

MEAN IQ SCORE OF AMISH PUPILS IN GRADES 5 TO 8 AND OF CONTROL
GROUP FOR GRADE 8, SRA TESTS OF EDUCATIONAL ABILITY

| Skills Tested | Amish Pupils Grade | | | | Control Group Grade |
	5 (N=30)	6 (N=67)	7 (N=91)	8 (N=115)	8 (N=61)
Language	86.7	86.8	89.2	91.1	99.4*
Reasoning	96.4	97.5	100.3	103.1	102.4
Quantitative	110.0	104.2	101.2	102.6	98.1
Composite score	96.7	94.7	94.4	96.7	99.5

* Difference between means for eighth grade were computed: P < .01.

TABLE 2

MEAN ACHIEVEMENT SCORES OF AMISH PUPILS IN GRADE 5 TO 8
AND OF CONTROL GROUP IN GRADE 8, IOWA TESTS OF BASIC SKILLS

| Skills Tested | Amish Pupils Grade | | | | Control Group Grade |
	5 (N=55)	6 (N=67)	7 (N=91)	8 (N=115)	8 (N=61)
Vocabulary	−1.32	−1.70	−1.48	−1.81	−0.92*
Comprehension	−0.73	−1.33	−1.09	−1.23	−1.19
Reference material	−0.78	−0.74	−0.68	−0.78	−0.77
Spelling	0.06	−0.09	·0.39	0.36**	−1.01
Word usage	0.71	0.22	0.43	0.16*	−1.52
Arithmetic	0.55	0.58	1.01	0.85*	−0.55

The norm of the Iowa test is 0.00. Deviations (plus or minus) from the norm are shown in years and months. For example, a score of 1.70 is equal to one year and seven months above the norm. Tests of significance between means are computed for eighth grade pupils.
* P < .01
** P < .05

Amish in all-Amish public schools, Amish pupils in public schools with non-Amish children, pupils in the control group, and non-Amish who attended the same schools as the Amish (Hostetler 1969:170). This pattern of success on the Iowa Tests of Basic Skills attests to the adequacy of the Amish schools.

The generally low performance of the Amish on the language aspects of the two tests described above can perhaps be attributed in part to the time limitation. On rechecking the reading tests we found that the children did very well in the part they finished; but, especially in the upper grades, most of the children who had not been trained to take timed tests did not complete the work. It should also be remembered that English is a second language that is not learned until they enter school.

Stanford Achievement Test   For comparison we obtained from public school records the Stanford Achievement Test scores for Amish and non-Amish pupils in a large geographic area in the Midwest. Scores were available for the first six grades. The Amish and non-Amish scores were about equal in most areas; however, here too the Amish made slightly higher scores in arithmetic than did the non-Amish.

Draw-a-Man Test   (The Goodenough-Harris Draw-a-Man Test. Dale B. Harris, *Children's Drawings as Measures of Intellectual Maturity*. New York: Harcourt, Brace & World, Inc., 1963.) This test was chosen to measure nonverbal in-

| Man | Woman | Self |

Drawings by boy age 10.

| Man | Woman | Self |

Drawings by girl age 10.

Drawings by children in Amish schools, from Goodenough-Harris Draw-a-Man Test, reflect traditional Amish values and patterns.

telligence. In addition to measuring intelligence, the test provides insights into
cultural influences, ability to form concepts, and ability to conceptualize relationships. It has been widely used, as Harris (1964) reports, in nonliterature cultures.
The test requires the pupil to draw a man, a woman, and himself. The man drawings
were scored, using 100 as a mean standard IQ measure.

The test was given to 389 pupils between the ages of 6 and 15 in Amish schools,
and the results were compared to U.S. norms. Only the drawing of a man has been

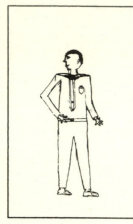  

| Man | Woman | Self |

Drawings by girl age 13.

| Man | Woman | Self |

Drawings by boy age 14.

*Drawings by Amish children in public schools, from Goodenough-Harris
Draw-a-Man Test. Amish children who attend public school identify
more with "alien" values than do children who attend Amish schools.*

validated as an indicator of intelligence. We used the drawings of a woman and self to gain additional insights into cultural factors. The Amish pupils in 12 Amish schools had a combined intelligence score of 101.6. The 12 schools ranged from a low 91.5 to a high of 112.7. The achievement in this test in the various Amish schools paralleled the degree of taboo against representing the human figure in the various communities. In spite of this taboo, pupils in Amish schools scored from 4.3 to 10.3 points higher than those Amish who attended public schools.

Whether the human figure was drawn with Amish or non-Amish characteristics presumably made no difference in the scores. An analysis of the drawings for such cultural influences, however, proved interesting. Differences were found between the drawings of the sexes. Amish boys in public school drew English-like (non-Amish) persons more frequently than did the girls. Amish girls were much more reserved in the use of English features in their drawing of the human figure. This difference in the sexes is consistent with what we know about the acculturation patterns in Amish culture, namely, that men are more exposed to, and are probably more at ease in, the outer world than are women. Pupils in Amish schools drew persons in Amish dress far more than did Amish pupils who attended public school. Occasionally an Amish child in public school would even draw himself as non-Amish. The drawings from the Amish schools clearly reflect the traditional culture. Amish pupils in public schools identify more with English or alien role models and values than the children in the Amish schools.

SUMMARY: PERSONALITY AND ACHIEVEMENT PATTERNS

The Amish personality type may be described as quiet, responsible, and conscientious. The Amishman works devotedly to meet his obligations, and although careful with detail, he needs time to master technical subjects. He is not especially good at working rapidly with complicated tasks. He likes to do things well. The Amish modal personality is loyal, considerate, sympathetic. The Amishman is concerned with how other people feel, even when they are in the wrong. He dislikes telling people unpleasant things. These personality endowments correspond generally with the values stressed in Amish culture.

Amish children tend to be very aware of other people, they prefer a certain amount of routine, and they relate well to most people. Their drawings reveal preferences for work-related activities; they do not make a sharp distinction between what is work and what is play. Happy-time activities reveal no rigid differentiation between the sexes. Drawings of the Amish home, as the children see it, include a variety of colors, often several buildings, and a spatial orientation of the farm environment that includes roads, gardens, and fences. The drawings reveal a realistic sense of environment, an ability to conceptualize space at an early age, and a strong identification of the individual with the home. The inclusion of others in their drawings suggests the importance of family and group activities.

The vocational preferences of Amish children are for service occupations and manual work. The children emulate the work roles of adults. Amish boys generally prefer farming or farm-related work. Girls prefer housekeeping, gardening, cooking, cleaning, caring for children, or some type of service, such as nursing or teaching. Their vocational aspirations are realistic and attainable within the limits of Amish culture. As judged by educational testing standards the overall performance of the Amish is similar to that of a representative sample of rural school children in the United States. In spite of the limited exposure the Amish children have to radio, television, and modern school facilities and although the Amish teachers themselves have had only an eighth-grade education, the Amish pupils scored significantly higher in spelling, word usage, and arithmetic than the pupils in our sample of rural public schools. They scored slightly above the national norm in these subjects in spite of small libraries and limited equipment. The Amish pupils were equal to the non-Amish pupils in comprehension and in the use of reference material. They scored lowest in vocabulary. (No tests were given in German vocabulary.) In those aspects of learning stressed by the Amish culture, the Amish pupils outperformed pupils in the control group. These findings are suggestive rather than conclusive. The Amish culture provides an environment for its children that is rather sharply delineated from the social climate of our Western civilization. By outside standards this environment is limiting and restricting, but to the Amish child it provides reasonable fulfillment and a knowledge of what is expected of him. Learning is directed toward conformity with a knowledge of what is right, rather than toward questioning existing knowledge or discovering new knowledge.

In any future concerted effort at educational testing, it must be remembered that no one can better judge what is good for the Amish community than the Amish themselves. Any effort to increase creativity or raise performance on standardized school tests among the Amish cannot be undertaken without also introducing the risk of cultural discontinuities. The introduction of greater competitive goals, resulting in greater appeal to self-interest and to self-importance, can only mean in Amish terms the loss of "humility, simple living, and resignation to the will of God."

7 / The government
and Amish schools

CONFRONTATION

EARLY ON A BRISK November morning in 1965, a school bus in Olwein, Iowa, headed for the Old Order Amish settlement a few miles to the southwest. Aboard were a driver, a school nurse, a truant officer, and the superintendent of schools. Their mission was to round up some 40 Amish children and bring them to Hazelton public school against the wishes of their parents and the leaders of the Amish church-community. Such decisive action was deemed necessary because the "plain people" had been violating the law by staffing their private one-room country schools with uncertified teachers. (Accounts appear in Erickson 1969:15–59 and Rodgers 1969.)

As the bus made the round of Amish homes, the delegation of public school officials encountered various forms of resistance. One farmer blocked his driveway to prevent the bus from entering. The superintendent entered the house and declared that, acting under the authority of Iowa's truancy statute, he had come to take the children to public school. The superintendent's efforts were of no avail. Some parents reported that the children were "not here," and others had sent them to the Amish school. After the last home had been visited, the public school officials drove to the Amish school, where many of the pupils had already arrived. By the time classes were scheduled to begin, the sheriff and the county attorney were also on the scene along with a number of parents and children.

The truant officer entered the building and explained his mission to the pupils. Declaring that he was their friend, that he wished to help them, and that they would receive a warm welcome in the town school, he asked them to be good children and quietly file into the bus behind the sheriff. The sheriff started slowly toward the bus, and the boys and girls followed. Suddenly, either the teacher or one of the mothers shouted in German, "Run!" The pupils bolted for the rear of the schoolyard, scrambled through the barbed-wire fence, and ran through the adjoining cornfield into the woods beyond. Some did not stop running until they reached their homes. Only two children failed to escape. A portly 13-year-old boy who could not keep up with his peers waddled confusedly into the arms of the deputy sheriff, who led the weeping youngster to the bus. A tiny girl of 6 never

97

got beyond the cornfield, where she shivered and screamed. The superintendent took her to a heated automobile and tried to calm her. The delegation of school officials decided to return to Olwein without the Amish children.

On the return to town that Friday morning, the truant officer suggested that "since the Hookies pulled a fast one on us, we should pull a fast one on them." (The Amish, who fasten their clothing with hooks-and-eyes because of their opposition to "ornaments," were called Hooks or Hookies by their Iowa neighbors.) That afternoon, when the parents were not about, the officials returned to the schools and succeeded in taking 28 children to the town school.

When the school officials returned on Monday to bus the children to town, they were met with resistance. The Amish had in the meantime secured the advice of an attorney. When the bus and its delegation arrived at the Amish school, they found the driveway blocked with a large horse-drawn wagon. The attorney for the Amish stood nearby and, reading from a legal document, made it known that anyone except the truant officer entering the private school grounds was liable for trespass. The truant officer retorted that he was allowed to bring assistants; the sheriff, who was also present, stated that he was responsible for upholding the law. He moved the wagon so that the bus could enter.

Guarding the school door were a group of stern-faced fathers. The sheriff and school officials pushed their way past the men—the Amish are pacifists—into the anteroom full of weeping mothers, who pulled at the sheriff's clothing and begged him to desist. He brushed them aside and stepped into the schoolroom proper. At that moment, the pupils began singing half-hysterically chorus after chorus of "Jesus Loves Me," led by a teacher who circled the room in distress. The superintendent attempted to pry a screaming schoolboy loose from a desk. Utter bedlam ensued as mothers rushed in to embrace their children protectively. Fathers entered to express their determination. The county attorney shouted his disgust at the way the Amish were behaving. So great was the turmoil that the authorities realized it would be impossible to effect a peaceful transfer of the children to public school. They retreated outdoors, and later that morning flew to the state capital for assistance from the state department of education. Behind them, they left an Old Order Amish community in a state of shock.

The Iowa incident is not an isolated case. For a number of years the Old Order Amish in other states have been arrested, jailed, and sentenced for not complying with school codes that adversely affect their church-community. Amishman LeRoy Garber, whose case the U.S. Supreme Court declined to hear, was harassed out of the state of Kansas for not enrolling his daughter in a public high school. Another Kansas Amishman, Adin Yutzy, paid a large fine, sold his farm, and moved to Wisconsin to get away from "school trouble." When Wisconsin began prosecuting the Amish for not sending their ninth-grade children to public high school, the Yutzy family moved to Missouri. The school conflict has resulted in jailings for many parents. They have generally been released after friends and businessmen paid their fines. Sympathetic attorneys who have taken cases to courts have generally found no relief. In Kentucky, however, a jury found the Amish not guilty of violating the school attendance laws because "they acted on the basis of religious conscience."

Amish parents in Wisconsin were convicted and fined in 1968 for not enrolling their children in the local high school. The trial court held that although the compulsory school law did interfere with their sincere religious beliefs, the law was "a reasonable constitutional exercise of a governmental function of the state." In reviewing the case, the Supreme Court of the State of Wisconsin (1970, Nos. 92, 93, 94) took a very different position. The court ruled that "there is no such a compelling state interest in two years high school compulsory education as will justify the burden it places upon the appellants' free exercise of their religion. To force a worldly education on all Amish children, the majority of whom do not want or need it, in order to confer a dubious benefit on the few who might later reject their religion is not a compelling interest."

In 1955 Amish leaders and state officials in Pennsylvania worked out an amicable agreement that permitted the operation of vocational schools (see Chapter 5). A more detailed agreement went into effect in Indiana in 1967 (Wells 1967). Michigan passed a bill that allows "the State Board of Education to set a definition for 'qualified personnel' as well as 'certified' teachers, a distinction which might let the board satisfy the Amish families (by allowing them to hire an Amish teacher) and also meet state laws." There has been no real trouble for Amish students in South Carolina, New York, Illinois, Missouri, Delaware, and Maryland. Maryland passed a bill stating that the Amish were a "bona fide church organization" and therefore not subject to license by the state. The Amish in Missouri report that the school officials are cooperative: "In our area we have had the nice cooperation of our local school board and the superintendent of the newly consolidated school district. They have sold us two good schoolhouses and most of the contents, just what we needed to get started." This is in strong contrast to the treatment the Amish received in Wayne County, Ohio, when a school board refused to sell the Amish an obsolete schoolhouse, even when there were no other buyers.

The laws in the various states pertaining to the public control of private schools show a surprising lack of uniformity. In most New England states there is no regulation of private elementary and secondary education other than that the building must be declared safe by the state fire marshal and it must have adequate toilets, sanitary drainage, and a safe water supply. In contrast, many midwestern states have detailed regulations on compulsory attendance, certification of teachers, the curricula to be taught, and, in some instances, subjects not to be taught. Despite these regional variations, there are seven areas in which agreement must be reached between the state governments and the Amish: (1) health and safety standards, (2) length of the school year, (3) length of the school day, (4) attendance requirements for enrolled pupils, (5) age of compulsory attendance, (6) certification of teachers, and (7) curricular requirements.

All states have certain building requirements pertaining to the health and safety of the children. The Amish cooperate cheerfully with these except when they go against specific religious prohibitions. Certain Amish church districts, for example, forbid indoor plumbing. These schools have outhouses similar in type to those built by the state at roadside and state parks. Electricity is forbidden in Amish homes and is not installed in the schools. Otherwise, all the safety measures are carefully followed.

THE SCHOOL YEAR

The minimum length of the public school year is determined by the state. For example, Ohio requires 160 days; Indiana, 167; Pennsylvania, 180. Some states require that nonpublic schools have the same length of year as neighboring public schools. The Amish believe in a short year, with most of the hours spent in school during the winter, when farm chores are not pressing. They prefer to begin school late in August and to eliminate vacations so they can close in April. Most schools have only two days off for Christmas, one day off for Thanksgiving, and one for Good Friday. A few may close on Easter Monday. Snow rarely closes an Amish school, for most of the pupils walk or come by horse and buggy or sleigh. Schools may be closed as required for major community events. Thus, the school may close when there is a funeral, for sometimes two-thirds of the children will be direct descendants of an old patriarch, and the rest will probably be related to him by marriage. More rarely the school may close for a wedding if the families of most of the schoolchildren are involved. If weather conditions cause cornhusking to fall behind schedule, the school may close for two or three days so the children can help with the harvest. These days are always made up, occasionally on Saturdays.

The reasons the Amish prefer a short school year are best described in their own words:

First: Although we appreciate having our own schools and teachers of our choice, we feel this still does not quite come up to having children together as a family unit under the influence of the parents. Having one more month of school would mean less family influence.

Second: Although we are a rural people in general, we realize there is a greater and greater need for a sound basic education. However, the old adage, "We learn to do by doing," still holds true. Learning from books becomes more meaningful as we tie it in with practical experience. During that last month of school our children would miss much of the basic principles of farming, that of preparing for and planting fields and gardens.

Third: We feel that our actual hours of classroom study in eight months would compare favorably with the average public school term of nine months. That is, counting such things as recreation during school sessions, basketball games, spring vacation, etc. . . .

Fourth: The nine-month school term is mainly intended for town and city children. We feel the extra month of school for us is not only unnecessary, but creates a burden and hardship to our way of life, in a spiritual as well as a material sense. We support our own schools, and at the same time support the public schools. This means higher taxes for us, and we are deprived of the help of our children at a time of year when we most need them.

Fifth: We feel that farming with tractors is not only impractical financially on most of our small farms, but with tractor farming we also tend to become more independent of each other, and lose much of the community spirit so essential for love and Christian fellowship in everyday life, as well as in the church.

Neither we nor our school system is perfect, but it is our aim to raise and educate our children to be not only good Christian stewards, faithful to God and our church, but also to be useful citizens in our community. For this privilege we are willing to continue supporting the public schools through our taxes, and to assume the financial responsibility ourselves of educating our children (Eli Gingerich, *Blackboard Bulletin*, August, 1966).

The length of the school day is determined in cooperation with the local officials. The Amish children generally attend school five to six hours a day, not including the lunch period. The vocational school children work on their academic studies or home projects five to six hours per day during school hours, and attend classes with a vocational teacher one-half to one full day per week.

ATTENDANCE

Regular attendance is required by the states of all schoolchildren. The Amish are cooperative about the attendance requirement for elementary school. Most Amish schools maintain an average attendance of well over 90 percent; the Indiana Amish have agreed to maintain an average attendance of 97 percent and to make up all the days when such an average is not maintained. When such pressing community work as cornhusking requires the children's help, the school closes rather than tolerate a series of absences. Then the missed days are made up. In such a closely-knit community it is impossible for a family to keep a child home to work without everyone knowing the real reason. In one community where this happened the teacher spoke to the parents, but after a while the child began missing again, so the school board spoke to them. They were warned that the child would be transferred to the public school if they did not fully cooperate. The parents once again kept the boy out of school, so he was transferred, whereupon the family got a retired doctor to sign a medical excuse and presented it to the public school, saying the boy was not healthy enough to attend. He continued to work both at home and for other families. The parents did not try to submit a doctor's excuse to the Amish school, for the community members would have known it was not valid. Needless to say, this is an unusual case, but it illustrates that the Amish schools are better able than the public schools to police their children. In most instances, even families that might be tempted to keep an older child at home for work do so very infrequently because they are sensitive to community pressure. Enforcing school attendance is no longer a problem at Amish elementary schools.

THE COMPULSORY AGE

The states determine compulsory school age. This has been the basis of much of the trouble between the Amish and the civil government. It was the major area of conflict in Pennsylvania and Ohio, a cause for concern in Indiana, Illinois, and Oklahoma, and resulted in litigation in Kansas, Kentucky, and Wisconsin. It is a point on which the Amish will not compromise; they will suffer fines or jail sentences and will migrate before they will capitulate. The Amish know that adolescence is a crucial age in the socialization of their children; they will not allow them to be socialized by the world during this formative period. They must shelter their children, not so much from ideas as from learning the roles and rules of the alien or English culture. The Amish understand intuitively what Lynd and Lynd pointed out so well in *Middletown* (1929:211–224; also Jules Henry 1963: 182–282), that the non-academic life of the public high school admirably prepares the students for social participation in American culture. The Amish therefore consider the high school to be a dangerous environment that is "a detriment to both farm and religious life." Not only do the children learn things they should not learn when they attend high school, they are also prevented from learning things they must know in order to live a successful life within the Amish community. The Amish solution is to operate their own vocational school.

The Amish believe that children who will be farmers and farmers' wives must enjoy physical work and must have the technical skills and knowledge to do their jobs well. These attitudes and skills cannot be learned in a classroom, but must be learned on the job. A boy learns to plow by plowing, by knowing the condition of the soil, the degrees of moisture, the weight of the plow, the temperament of the horses. He learns how to plow a long, straight furrow, when to plow and when to wait for the soil to dry a little, whether to plow or disk. All of this is best learned by doing rather than sitting at a desk reading about it. He needs to develop physical skill, stamina, and a great deal of judgment. These can only be developed by repeated experience. In the same way the girl needs to learn how to prepare the soil for her vegetable garden, what to plant, when and how to plant it, how to care for the growing vegetables, when and how to pick them, and then how to prepare and preserve them so they will be in peak condition for future use. The 45-minute home economics classes in the local high school seem pretty superficial, compared to the experience the Amish girl acquires in her own community.

CERTIFICATION AND CURRICULA

Only six states require that teachers in nonpublic schools be certified. The Amish have schools in three of them, and in two of these, Iowa and Michigan, certification has been a source of trouble. The roughshod attempt at enforcement of the certification law by Iowa school officials resulted in protests from all parts of the nation (Erickson 1969). Amish schools are still in operation in Iowa and Michigan, but their continuation depends almost as much on public support as on the limited legal safeguards that have been granted them (Rodgers 1969:89).

Although Ohio is not one of the states that require teachers in nonpublic schools to be certified, the department of education officials interpreted the Ohio Law, "a child not attending a public school must attend a school which meets the state board of education standards" (Ohio Legislative Service Commission 1960:5) to mean that "teachers in private schools must have the same certification as teachers in tax-supported schools." The state has prosecuted Amish parents under this interpretation of the law. However, the state officials did not receive as much public support for their action as they wished, and no further legal cases have occurred during the last few years. Amish schools are barely tolerated by the state authorities and lack of prosecution is primarily the result of sympathetic publc opinion. Although Indiana, like Ohio, does not require teacher certification in nonpublic schools, the state closed an Amish school in Decatur County by using the argument that a teacher with less than 10 years of formal schooling could not provide educational training equivalent to that provided by the public schools. As part of their agreement with the state education authorities (Wells 1967), the Indiana Amish consented to have as teachers only individuals who pass the eighth grade satisfactorily and make a passing score on the General Educational Development High School Equivalency Test administered and graded by the State Department of Public Instruction. Because the civil government and the Amish measure the teacher by different standards, almost all teachers who are certified by the state are not considered qualified by Amish standards.

Thirty-one states regulate the curricula of nonpublic schools either by specifically defining course requirements or by demanding various measures of equivalence between nonpublic and public school instruction (Erickson 1969:104). But even in states like Ohio and Michigan, where statutory standards include lengthy specifications, public officials have sometimes exceeded the intent of the law, as when they tried to close Amish schools. The officials report that the statutory power is too vague to enforce the curriculum standards in nonpublic schools. The major question is: Who is to determine equivalency? Iowa has had the most detailed and restrictive policy concerning the curriculum to be taught in Amish schools. In order to be permitted to maintain a school, "proof of achievement in the basic skills of arithmetic, the communicative arts of reading, writing, grammar, and spelling, and an understanding of United States history, history of Iowa, and the principles of American government . . . shall be determined on the basis of tests or other means of evaluation selected by the state superintendent with the approval of the board" (Iowa Senate file 785, July, 1967).

The Indiana School Agreement specifies courses to be taught in the elementary school. "Minimum Standards for the Amish Parochial Schools of Ohio" (Hershberger 1960) lists graded courses of study: language arts (including reading, writing, spelling, and English), mathematics, geography and history, health and safety rules, vocal music, and German writing, reading and spelling. The Amish in several other states follow the Ohio minimum standards. The curriculum for the vocational schools is specified in more or less detail by the different states in which Amish live; in some states there is no specific agreement but, as yet, a quiet tolerance.

The Amish conscientiously attempt to obey all these school regulations, for they believe that the government is instituted by God and that Christians should be obedient to the government in all things that are not in direct conflict with the laws of God. They honor government officials and pray for them. They also pray for their own children, whom they fear the government's school may "take out of their hands and turn into men of the world."

It is obvious that the Amish will not tolerate the removal of their children to a distance from their homes, where they are placed in large groups with narrow age limits, taught skills that are useless to their way of life, and exposed to values and attitudes antithetical to their own. These conditions develop when schools become large and bureaucratic. Then the Amish withdraw or migrate, for they say "it is better to suffer than to compromise." They establish their own schools, and when that is not possible, they move to other states or even to other countries. Two Amish groups recently left the United States for Central America in search of more freedom to raise their children in keeping with their ideals. Another settlement of Amish was founded in Paraguay, and several new communities have been formed in Canada. The Amish are determined to raise their children to thrive on coopera-tion and humility, rather than competition and pride of achievement.

In the United States the Old Order Amish are granted a tenuous permission, revokable virtually at the whim of the state superintendents, to maintain their own schools. It is national public opinion, not school officials or state legislatures, that enables the Amish to keep their own schools in operation.

8 / Perspectives on Amish education

EDUCATION HAS BEEN highly valued in the United States, if not for its intrinsic worth, at least for its effect on an individual's status. An adequate education is considered the right of every child and justified concern is expressed for children who are educationally deprived. When the Old Order Amish began to withdraw from the public school system to set up their own private schools, neighbors and state officials alike believed that it would be impossible for them to give their children an adequate education. The schools were small, with limited equipment; neither their teachers nor their school board members had been graduated from high school; and the schools were completely financed and administered by the local Amish community. Is adequate education possible under such circumstances? We studied the total Amish culture—the community, the family, and the school—and then selected a sample of Amish schools in various communities in North America for intensive study, including administering standardized tests. One of the criteria for school selection was that the teacher should be experienced, having taught not less than three years, and be considered a good teacher by the Amish community. We concluded that these Amish community schools are successful when judged by public school standards (standardized tests), when judged by independent school certification standards (goal attainment), and when judged by the traditional Old Order Amish community.

The Amish schools are more successful than specialized government schools for minority groups (such as the schools on Indian reservations), where local cultures contribute little to the school and are not identified with the educational system. They are more successful than many ghetto schools in which middle-class culture rather than the children's experiences determines teachers' attitudes and techniques. They are more successful for Amish children than consolidated schools, for they enable the Amish children not only to master the requisite academic material, but also to develop a positive self-image within their own culture and at the same time to identify with American culture without emulating its total likeness.

Although the Amish schools are admirably suited to the needs of the Amish children and similar schooling might be utilized by other groups within our society, Amish-type schools could not meet the needs of major segments of the population in the United States. By design, Amish schools are not suited for training artists, musicians, painters, and actors; nor for training science-oriented in-

105

dividuals who would pursue engineering, astronomy, palaeontology, chemistry, or space technology; nor for training business executives, corporation managers, or occupations leading to government and military careers. The Amish school, by intent, does not function as an institution for upward mobility in the modern industrial complex.

EDUCATION FOR PERSISTENCE AND EDUCATION FOR CHANGE

Contemporary Western society is faced with an unprecedented explosion of population and technology. When educating the increasing number of children to live in an increasingly complex society based somewhat precariously on a natural environment that is rapidly being modified by man, the question arises as to the balance between an education for persistence and an education for change. Should the children be taught about things as they were and are, in the belief that there will not be really basic changes, at least on the level of physical and psychological needs? Or should the children's education lead them to expect and seek change? Obviously there must be some balance, for a knowledge of the past and an understanding of our cultural heritage is helpful in determining both the direction and

Hitching rail with parking meters accommodates the Amish customers in a rural town (A Fred Wilson Photo).

acceptance of change. A humanistic tradition is needed to prevent technology from being used against man. The conflict between the Amish and the public schools is in the area of emphasis in education. The public schools, especially since the Gaither Report of 1957, have been overwhelmingly committed to the teaching of science. Recent Supreme Court rulings severely limiting the role of religion in public education have made it more difficult for the public schools to teach traditional values. New teaching methods and materials are designed to enhance individual learning, to teach intellectual concepts, and to develop initiative and creativity within fairly wide boundaries. Children are encouraged to seek new ways of doing things in order to meet the challenge of our times. In the absence of definite proof the new way is considered to be better than the old way.

In contrast the Amish emphasize education for persistence. Although the Amish show remarkable resourcefulness in adjusting to the changing culture around them, it is a resourcefulness that enables them to maintain their traditional world view and their traditional way of life rather than to bring these into line with the changing technical and social environment. In the absence of definite proof, the old way is considered to be better than the new way.

The Amish school is benevolently authoritarian; the teacher is the shepherd, the children are the flock. Her authority is natural, for it derives from the parents and the community and from her role as protector and source of certitude and approval. Her authority is not arbitrary and is not based on intimidation. The Amish children are taught that there are right answers for all questions, even if they or the teacher may not know them. There is right and wrong, and it is more important to do what is morally right than it is to win acclaim, popularity, or riches, or to survive physically. In order to decide what is morally right, one looks to the Bible, the *Ordnung*, and the elders—to the wisdom of the ages rather than to the pronouncements of modern science.

Within the clearly defined and relatively narrow boundaries of the culture and the school there is considerable freedom. There is a certain richness and diversity of experience in the small Amish school with its face-to-face organization and its long-term intimate relationships. Respect accrues to each individual if he does not exceed the boundaries. Thus, if a child is not good at softball or is slow at mastering spelling, he is not rejected or looked down on. Variation in ability is realistically accepted. Patterns of decision making and authority are clear. Many decisions are made by the teacher as representative of the community, but when the children are invited to participate in decision making, their views are respected. The basic conditions for education are possible with very limited educational equipment when the elements of trust, respect, and acceptance of honest needs and wishes are shared by the teacher and the pupils.

QUALIFIED TEACHERS AND CERTIFIED TEACHERS

The wisdom of the ages is better imparted to children by example than by precept. Therefore the Amish feel very strongly that the teachers in their schools should be participating members of the Amish culture. Since the Amish limit formal education of their members, although they encourage informal education, the Amish teachers do not meet state certification standards. The Amish reject certified teachers—teachers who have completed prescribed college course requirements—because teachers who meet state standards generally prefer the scientific method of analysis to the prescientific, oral tradition. They are not qualified by Amish standards and are incapable of teaching Amish children by the example of their lives. Because of the limited formal training of Amish teachers, there has been widespread concern about the quality of the teaching the children are receiving in the Amish schools. Our findings show that even though the teachers are not state certified, they are in fact qualified, and that the children are given a satisfactory education in the basic academic skills. (In their own schools, the Amish tested higher than the children in rural public schools in spelling, arithmetic, and word usage.) In addition, their education admirably prepares them for life as Amishmen in the twentieth century. The children aspire to the occupational roles available to them; they succeed in these roles and enjoy their chosen vocations. Their education enables them to be both Amishmen and Americans—to attain a comfortable identity as they perpetuate their distinctive way of life.

All elementary school children need role models. Learning is enhanced when the children can identify with the teacher and the teacher can identify with the children. A primary reason the Amish schools are successful is that the Amish teacher and children understand one another and identify with each other. Saltzman (1963:323) has pointed out that there is an important distinction between understanding and identification: understanding is cerebral and identification is visceral. Many educators may have the capacity to understand the needs of a community and the willingness to meet these needs, but fail to identify with either the community or the children. Where the social class (or culture) of the community and the teacher are similar, both understanding and identification are likely to exist. When teachers work in communities or in a culture whose dominant values they either hold or respect, and whose child-training practices they approve and tend to follow themselves, they are better able to teach effectively, to serve as examples to the children, and to help the children to grow culturally. Where middle-class teachers confront lower-class children and parents or where there are sharp differences in culture, ethnicity, or race, understanding may be possible but identification is halfhearted or largely unsuccessful. The oft-repeated notion of having the best teachers in the poorer schools may be pointless except where both the cerebral and visceral ability of the teachers are taken into account. To teach well, the teacher must be able to accept her pupils' need for cultural persistence as well as for cultural change.

The concept of "qualified teacher" in addition to that of "certified teacher" should be considered for schools serving other cultural groups. It has been suggested that selected black veterans might be encouraged to teach in ghetto elementary schools. These men would be chosen on the basis of personality, achievement, and ability rather than on specific educational background. They would be given a very short intensive course, perhaps of only a few weeks, before they began teaching. Similarly, Indian and Chicano teachers might also be incorporated into the local school system to help make the education relevant to the child being educated, to establish an atmosphere of respect between the teacher and the pupil, and to develop the vital parent-teacher relationship that has repeatedly been demonstrated to be essential for the effective education of the child. Individuals from the community might teach such culturally specialized skills as silverworking, indigenous music, legends, and minority cultural history. In other words, people with little formal education should be in certain cases welcomed into the classroom and acknowledged not only as satisfactory teachers, but as superior teachers. Teacher certification as generally practiced is too narrow, for it excludes those individuals who may be best qualified to identify with and teach children of culturally divergent groups. Teacher certification often excludes those individuals who can give the children enough of their own culture to make them sufficiently secure to be open to education for change.

EDUCATION FOR SOCIAL COHESION AND EDUCATION FOR TECHNOLOGICAL COMPETENCE

Education for social cohesion and education for technological competence are both essential. We do not want to produce, in Justice Robert Jackson's words, "technically competent barbarians," nor can we afford to neglect the technical training that is essential if human resources and the resources of the environment are to be utilized in such a manner as to provide a good life for successive generations. If social cohesion is to be developed organically and not imposed by a master technology, then certain educational methods seem to be applicable. For example, in teaching technical competence, the subject matter is the controlling influence, rather than the style of life of the teacher or the students' personal relation to the teacher. An extremely asocial and difficult genius might contribute more technical know-how than a number of intuitive and gifted teachers, but more than the facts are necessary to motivate people to want to live in a style that is not just socially acceptable but is socially responsible.

The Amish stress social responsibility in the education of their children. Social cohesiveness rather than intellectual creativity or critical analysis is the goal of Amish schooling. Therefore, in Amish schools the emphasis on values generally supersedes the emphasis on facts. However, factual material, though somewhat circumscribed, is learned thoroughly. Amish children are taught both by practice and by example to care for and support the members of the school and the community. Under teacher supervision children teach one another within the same grade and across grades. The school children visit the sick and help the elderly and are visited at school by adults of the local community and travelers from distant Amish communities.

The Amish are not committed to the assumption that legitimate forms of learning are primarily abstract and analytical. They believe that learning should be practical and should lead to a disciplined life on earth, concern for others, and an eternity in heaven. In their educational program they utilize drill and rote learning that will lead to shared knowledge and social success.

In addition to the Amish there are other ethnic and linguistic communities whose culture is primarily oral rather than literary, interpersonal rather than impersonal, relationally oriented rather than analytically oriented. Our study of Amish socialization, and particularly the results of the Myers-Briggs Type Indicator, clearly suggest the ineptness of preparing these children for analytically related vocations. We suspect that the same would be true of other cultures of the oral tradition type. The extraordinarily high scores of the Amish in the area of sensing and feeling are consistent with their ability to relate to others, with their sense of social cohesiveness, and with their face-to-face group structure. The Amish children manifest trusting rather than alienated relationships and therefore possess psychological strengths that should not be undermined by an educational system that is primarily competitive, analytical, and technologically oriented. They will flourish when the educational subject matter is presented in a style that is consistent with the positive aspects of their world view. This does not mean that they are getting a second-class education nor that they are being prevented from entering the mainstream of American culture; rather their psychological strength is being maintained while they learn the facts and an approach to education that will make it possible, should the individual so choose, to continue his education beyond that offered by his own culture.

The Amish children scored lowest in vocabulary and language on the standardized tests. This suggests, among other explanations, a strong tie to oral in contrast to literary values in their tradition. The limitation in vocabulary and language as measured by standardized tests may be seen as a part of the larger value pattern of nonexposure to the world and is thus part of the "good life" as defined by the Amish charter. It is an aspect of separation from the world. Aside from any ambiguity in the standardized tests that might account for Amish score performance, we must remember that the Amish demand economy of words, slowness in mastering content, and prohibitions against showmanship in the use of vocabulary. Moderation is a life principle learned throughout the school years; consideration for others outweighs individual achievement.

Our findings suggest a similarity to children studied in other subcultures whose cognitive style is primarily relational rather than analytic (Cohen 1969:842). If these children are to develop marketable skills, they will require, according to Friedenberg (1970:43), instruction by techniques that emphasize drill and rote learning. Drill and rote learning, especially when carried on in a group, are more of a social activity than is analysis or abstract thinking, which is primarily an individual exercise. Children whose world view is based on an oral tradition and a personal appropriation of group memory and group wisdom rather than on scientific analysis and abstract reasoning should not be deprived of learning methods that utilize memorization. It is not that these children are without curiosity, it is rather that their curiosity is prescientific and is often social and practical rather than technological. Certainly within our culture we have need for those who appropriate old skills as well as for those who invent new ones.

The Amish are basically nonexploitative both of individuals and of natural resources. People are not conceived of in terms of work units or manpower, nor is the physical environment believed to be inexhaustible. Social responsibility extends beyond concern for their people to stewardship of the land. They consciously reject the goals of a society that is "hung up on competitive achievement" (Friedenberg 1970:43) and that stresses efficiency above all else. Manipulation and power over others is denounced; nurturing and the bearing of one anothers' burdens are encouraged.

One of the methods by which the Amish teach and maintain social cohesion is by keeping the units of the church and the school small, so that both function on a face-to-face basis without dependence on administration. The Amish simplify their life by keeping their institutions on a human rather than a bureaucratic scale. Their personal relationships involve repeated encounters and generally persist over a long period of time. There is a homogeneity of belief that makes consensus possible. When homogeneity is lost, the church or the school divides into smaller units. Within the Amish school the children are in a single group in which everyone knows everyone else, in which every family knows every other family, and in which the teacher not only knows all the children but also all the children's families. Often the children have the same teacher for several years and her life is intermixed with theirs in the life of the church and the community. Such a school is not merely a place of instruction, but is part of the children's whole life and culture. It is an ideal environment in which to transmit cultural attitudes. The teacher is in a good position to encourage moral thoughtfulness and to lead frank discussions of social behavior when problems of meanness, fighting, or lying occur.

Young children seem to be able to learn most easily in an environment where they feel secure and where they are accepted as individuals. Dennison (1969:12, 29), in describing the First Street School, pointed out that the small face-to-face nature of the school diminished anxiety; he makes a plea for the establishment of "mini-schools" that are characterized by intimacy and small scale. Although the teaching methods used in the First Street School were totally different from those used in Amish schools, both types of school are characterized by intimate contacts among children and teachers and a real respect for individuality. Children learn social cohesion by experience within a socially cohesive group.

It should be pointed out that education for social cohesion and education for technological competence need not be opposed to one another, although in school practice it sometimes appears that they are. The styles in public education change with the needs—or imagined needs—of the surrounding culture. Thus the emphasis moved from social adjustment as urbanization spread to technological competence as we responded to Sputnik, and now there appears to be a need to reassess some of our educational practices in the light of man's relation to man, his relation to his physical environment, and the relation of one cultural group to another. Although the Amish schools have largely rejected scientific analysis and training in abstract reasoning, perhaps we can learn something from them in the fields of interpersonal relationships—nonexploitation of the environment, dedication to a principled world view, and the creation of an environment protected from shoddiness, violence, and treachery in which to nurture children and imbue them with a sense of responsibility for others.

VOCATIONAL TRAINING WITHIN THE ADULT WORLD

The Amish have devised a system of vocational training for their adolescents that takes them outside the school, into the world of adults, and into the life of the community in order that the young people may learn vocational roles as well as vocational skills. These are not "made" jobs, for the community needs their labor and is acutely conscious of its responsibility for training the young people. The students spend half a day a week in school under the direction of a teacher and four and a half days working in a modified apprentice system, generally under the direction of their parents. They are learning technological skills in a social context as participants in the economy of the community. While working on a family farm, Amish children of high school age learn not only how to perform a task, such as how to cut silage, but also when to cut it and how to integrate the cutting of the silage into all the other work that is required of the vocation "farmer." They also learn wider community work roles by helping in threshing rings and at cornhuskings, getting ready for church, and helping care for neighbors' children. The young people have practice interacting with the various people with whom they will work throughout their adult lives. Of great importance to the success of the Amish vocational training is that the vocational expectations of the young people coincide with the vocational opportunities available to them.

Adolescents learn faster by actual participation than by talking about participation. Working at real jobs outside the school walls helps students to envision their adult roles and their place in society. Were a program similar to the Amish vocational school program to be implemented by a public school, the selection of individuals to direct and train the students might pose a problem, for in our mobile and diversified society the children's parents would rarely be the ideal individuals to direct the training. It would also be more difficult to find meaningful work that was integrated into the community economy. A directed apprentice program could enable students to master the etiquette of the job by learning how to behave in relation to superiors and towards co-workers. With such a vocational program the young person could develop a realistic concept of the job role for which he was training; he would learn both the technological and the social aspects of his work.

There is an underlying assumption in the United States that academic achievement is the most important object of all schooling and that if the school reform does not affect academic achievement, it is worthless. Despite these assumptions "there is little evidence that academic competence is critically important to adults in most walks of life" (Jencks 1969). Most employers will not hire dropouts for reasons other than academic incompetence. It is for moral, social, and emotional reasons. Too often the dropouts do not get to work on time; they can not be counted on to do a careful job, can not be trusted with other people's property or goods, and can not get along well with others in the office or plant. The teaching of more history, verbal skills, or science will not suffice. What is needed is training in responsibility, self-discipline, and self-respect. These nonacademic traits can be taught in an apprentice system as well as in a classroom.

The Amish system of vocational education combines on-the-job training with academic work under a teacher's guidance and with peer group interaction at the weekly classes. The various social and cultural needs of the adolescent are met by this program. The young adult has an opportunity to relate to his family, his boss, his teacher, and his peers while contributing to the economic life of his community.

LOCAL CONTROL OF ELEMENTARY EDUCATION

For over 100 years the Amish chose to remain within the public school system. They did not establish their own schools until they were threatened by the mono-cultural public school that in essence would not grant them an identity of their own and would not permit them to be raised both as Amishmen and as Americans. As long as the public schools were small in size and on a human rather than an organizational scale—therefore local in character—the Amish exerted an influence in the public school as had the Swedes and Finns in other localities. As the administrative unit became larger through consolidation, small, culturally divergent groups were subordinated to the larger numbers of middle-class Americans and thereby lost their influence over the style, as well as the policies, of the schools that serve their children. Today most public schools are controlled by the middle class and reflect their culture regardless of the cultural composition of the students attending any particular school.

From our study of the Amish it appears that when the public school officials "recognize and honor responsible diversity" (Sizer 1969:42), then the needs of a minority cultural group can be met within the public school system. Where the Amish were successful in their attempt to modify the public school system, their children remained in the public school and thus continued to be taught by state-certified teachers. They were in an educational situation in which their distinctive culture was respected while they were at the same time introduced to aspects of middle-class American society. Where the state school officials remained rigid and made little attempt to understand or work with the Amish, the Amish withdrew completely from the public schools and built and staffed their own schools. They withdrew because of changes in public school philosophy and organization that threatened their cultural identity, not because they wanted to teach religion in the school. By Amish standards the public schools had become intolerable for their children. In a similar response, although the specifics of the situation are admittedly very different, the black community has decided that it must make the decisions about what can and can not be tolerated for their children in terms of public schooling. Other culture groups such as the Chinese, Japanese, and Jews have for generations countered the public schools by establishing supplementary schools to teach their language and culture to their children.

The Old Order Amish have demonstrated that not only are they able to make

a substantial contribution to policy making in local public schools when they are permitted to, but they can, when necessary, organize and staff their own schools without any outside help and despite discouraging legal suits initiated by the state. Our findings indicate that the Amish children in their own schools tested slightly (though not significantly) higher on achievement tests than those who were attending public schools. Perhaps the public school system could be improved by respecting cultural differences and encouraging members of minority groups to participate in the organization and implementation of their children's schooling. If members of their own cultural minority participated in the schools, Indian children might not suffer educationally and psychologically during their later school years (Murray Wax et al., 1964), and black children might not be as withdrawn and alienated from the school by the time they reach the upper elementary grades. A study of a London school in which 29 percent of the children were immigrants —from Cyprus, the West Indies, and Italy—indicated that parental involvement in the school, even when the parents were almost lacking in formal education and quite inarticulate in English, resulted in "small but significant improvement in some of the scores of the children when they were tested" (Lady Plowden, Introduction to Young and McGeeney, 1968). The fear of implementing local control or of involving parents in the school, especially when parents lack formal education, appears to be unfounded.

Our study illustrates that local control (in this case complete local control) with no funds or supplies from the government can work well even though the parents have a limited educational background (eight years of formal schooling), speak English as a second language, and are culturally different from the prevailing American culture. By "work well" we mean that the parents are satisfied with the schools, the children who graduate from them are well prepared for adult life, and, as judged by public school standards of success on standardized tests, the children are adequately taught.

EDUCATION IN A MULTICULTURAL SOCIETY

Contemporary research in education in the United States, including this study of the Amish, suggests that a rigid monocultural educational philosophy is neither viable nor desirable. The culture of the United States is becoming more homogeneous, due to such influences as the mass media, radio, television, and advertising. Cultural minorities are at the same time insisting on a say in their education. The increasing homogeneity of the larger culture lends by contrast greater visibility to the minority cultures. Minorities are simultaneously rejected by the dominant homogenizing culture. When there was greater isolation, a minority group could more easily retain its own identity; in fact there was little chance of losing it.

Unlike the Indian, the black, the Chicano, or the Puerto Rican, the Old Order Amish have suffered neither a profound cultural jolt nor a weakening of their self-image. Nor have they felt the need to change their identity. In assessing the role of education and self-identity it is important to remember that the blacks, and to a lesser extent the Indians and the Chicanos, are going through a process of community development involving a change of identity. What could better express their desire for a change than their insistence on using a new label to designate their people? The "Negroes" have become "blacks," and the "Mexican-Americans" are striving to be known as "Chicanos." In Goodenough's terms they are clearing their "social decks" so that they can do something positive about creating a new identity for themselves (Goodenough 1961:93). They do not want to be assimilated into the larger culture, but want instead to maintain the distinctive aspects of their own culture while participating in the economy of the dominant culture. The concept of the school as the pot in which the cultures melt works well for those who wish to—and who are able to—merge their identity with the American middle class, but for others the concept must be re-examined.

When culturally different children attend a school that teaches an unattainable identity, an identity that would demand the rejection of the values of the home, the tribe, or the street, and even the color of their skin, what can be the resultant self-image? When the child is forced to choose between the culture in which he has spent his first five years, the culture of the real life of the home and its environment, and the artificial and, to him, often meaningless culture of the school, he generally rejects the school and with it, all formal education.

The Amish have been able to stop, at least temporarily, the onslaught of the large school and its associated values. They have scant legal protection and little guarantee other than public sentiment for the maintenance of their schools, in which their children are learning the skills and attitudes required of their culture. Were it not for the Amish appeal to religious freedom and nostalgic American values, their communities would long since have been forced out of their pastoral "poverty" into the economic mainstream, where they would either have contributed more to the gross national product or would have added to the welfare rolls already swelled with unhappy individuals drifting between the culture they no longer have and the middle-class culture they do not fully embrace. Instead the Amish have been able, through community discipline and community support of their members and by the careful protection and nurture of their children, to maintain cultural continuity and cultural integrity, to remain a discrete minority, steadfast to their own vision of the good life.

Bibliography and references cited

BACHMAN, CALVIN G., 1942, *The Old Order Amish of Lancaster County, Pennsylvania*. Norristown, Pa.: Pennsylvania German Society (reprinted in 1961).

BEILER, AARON E., 1961, *Record of Principles Pertaining to the Old Order Amish Church Sect School Committee as of September 2, 1937. Reaffirmed and Approved through Counsel of the Committee August 9, 1961*. Gap, Pa.

BENEDICT, RUTH, 1957, *Patterns of Culture*. New York: Houghton Mifflin.

BERG, IVAR, 1970, *Education and Jobs: The Great Training Robbery*. New York: Praeger.

Blackboard Bulletin, The. Aylmer, Ontario: Pathway Publishing Corporation. Published monthly "in the interests of Amish parochial schools." Founded 1957.

BRONFENBRENNER, URIE, 1970, *Two Worlds of Childhood: U.S. and U.S.S.R.* New York: Russell Sage.

BUCHANAN, FREDERICK S., 1967, *The Old Paths: A Study of the Amish Response to Public Schooling in Ohio*. Ph.D. dissertation, Department of Education, Ohio State University.

BYLER, URIA R., 1963, *Our Better Country*. Gordonville, Pa.: Old Order Book Society.

———, 1969, *School Bells Ringing: A Manual for Amish Teachers and Parents*. Aylmer, Ontario: Pathway Publishing Corporation.

COHEN, ROSALIE A., 1969, "Conceptual Styles, Culture Conflict, and Nonverbal Tests of Intelligence," *American Anthropologist* 71:828–856.

COMMAGER, HENRY S., 1962, *Foreword to McGuffey's Sixth Eclectic Reader*. 1879 Edition. New York: Signet Classics.

DENNISON, GEORGE, 1969, *The Lives of Children: The Story of the First Street School*. New York: Random House.

EDUCATIONAL POLICIES COMMISSION, 1961, *The Central Purpose of Education*. Washington, D.C.: National Educational Association.

ERICKSON, DONALD A., 1968, "The 'Plain People' & American Democracy," *Commentary*, January, pp. 43–47.

———, 1969, *Public Controls for Non-Public Schools*. Chicago: University of Chicago Press.

ERIKSON, ERIK H., 1950, *Childhood and Society*. New York: Norton.

Family Life. Aylmer, Ontario: Pathway Publishing Corporation. A monthly "dedicated to the promotion of Christian living among the plain people, with special emphasis on the appreciation of our heritage." Founded January 1968.

FREED, RUTH S., AND STANLEY A. FREED, 1968, "Family Background and Occupational Goals of School Children of the Union Territory of Delhi, India," *American Museum Noviatates*, No. 2348, October 4. New York: American Museum of Natural History, pp. 1–39.

FRIEDENBERG, EDGAR Z., 1970, "The Real Functions of Educational Testing," *Change*, January–February, pp. 43–47.

GOODENOUGH, WARD, 1961, "Education and Identity," in *Anthropology and Education*, Frederick C. Gruber, ed. Philadelphia: University of Pennsylvania Press, pp. 84–102.

GOODMAN, MARY E., 1957, "Value, Attitudes, and Concepts of Japanese and American Children," *American Anthropologist* 59:979–999.

HARRIS, DALE B., 1963, *Children's D:awings as Measures of Intellectual Maturity*. New York: Harcourt.

HARRIS, DALE B., 1964, "A Cross-Cultural Analysis of Children's Drawings," Unpublished manuscript. University Park, Pa.: Pennsylvania State University.

HENRY, JULES, 1963, *Culture against Man*. New York: Random House.

———, 1963, "Spontaneity, Initiative, and Creativity in Suburban Classrooms," in *Education and Culture*, George D. Spindler, ed. New York: Holt, Rinehart and Winston, Inc., pp. 215–233.

———, 1969, "Is Education Possible? Are We Qualified to Enlighten Dissenters?" in *Public Controls for Non-Public Schools*, Donald A. Erickson, ed. Chicago: University of Chicago Press, pp. 83–102.

HERSHBERGER, HENRY J., 1960, *Minimum Standards for the Amish Parochial or Private Elementary Schools of the State of Ohio as a Form of Regulation. Compiled and Approved by Bishops, Committeemen and Others in Conference*. Apple Creek, Ohio, RR# 2.

HOLT, JOHN, 1964, *How Children Fail*. New York: Pitman.

HOSTETLER, J. A., 1968, *Amish Society*. Baltimore, Md.: The Johns Hopkins Press.

———, 1969, *Educational Achievement and Life Styles in a Traditional Society, the Old Order Amish*. Washington, D.C.: U.S. Department of Health, Education and Welfare. Final Report, Project No. 6-1921.

HOSTETLER, J. A., AND G. E. HUNTINGTON, 1967, *The Hutterites in North America*. New York: Holt, Rinehart and Winston, Inc.

HUNTINGTON, GERTRUDE ENDERS, 1956, *Dove at the Window: A Study of an Old Order Amish Community in Ohio*. Ph.D. dissertation, Yale University.

JENCKS, CHRISTOPHER, 1969, "A Reappraisal of the Most Controversial Educational Document of Our Times," *New York Times Magazine*, August 10, pp. 12 ff.

KOLLMORGEN, WALTER M., 1942, *Culture of a Contemporary Community: The Old Order Amish of Lancaster County, Pennsylvania*, Rural Life Studies, No. 4. Washington, D.C.: U.S. Department of Agriculture.

LEE, DOROTHY, 1959, *Freedom and Culture*. Englewood Cliffs, N.J.: Prentice-Hall.

———, 1963, "Discrepancies in the Teaching of American Culture," in *Education and Culture*, George D. Spindler, ed. New York: Holt, Rinehart and Winston, Inc.

LINTON, RALPH, 1945, *The Cultural Background of Personality*. New York: Appleton.

LITTELL, FRANKLIN H., 1964, *The Origins of Sectarian Protestantism*. New York: Macmillan.

LOOMIS, CHARLES P., AND J. ALLAN BEEGLE, 1950, *Rural Social Systems*. Englewood Cliffs, N.J.: Prentice-Hall.

LYND, R. S., AND H. M. LYND, 1929, *Middletown: A Study in Contemporary American Culture*. New York: Harcourt.

MILLER, WAYNE, 1969, *A Study of Amish Academic Achievement*. Ph.D. dissertation, Department of Education, University of Michigan.

MYERS, ISABELL B., 1962, *The Myers Briggs Type Indicator*. Princeton, N.J.: Educational Testing Service.

NIEBUHR, H. RICHARD, 1929, *The Social Sources of Denominationalism*. New York: Henry Holt and Company.

NISLEY, JONAS, 1965, *Children's Read, Write, Color, Book*. Baltic, Ohio: Author.

Ohio Legislative Service Commission, 1960, *Sectarian Amish Education.* Columbus, Ohio: Research Report No. 44.

Pathway Publishers, 1970, *Tips for Teachers, A Handbook for Amish Teachers.* Aylmer, Ontario, and Lagrange, Indiana.

Pathway Reading Series, 1968. Aylmer, Ontario: Pathway Publishing Corporation. Titles: *Thinking of Others* (Fifth Grade), *Step by Step* (Sixth Grade), *Seeking True Values* (Seventh Grade), and *Our Heritage* (Eighth Grade).

Pennsylvania Department of Public Instruction, 1955, "Policy for Operation of Home and Farm Projects in Church Organized Schools." Harrisburg, Pa.: October 5.

RODGERS, HARRELL R., 1969, *Community Conflict, Public Opinion and the Law: The Amish Dispute in Iowa.* Columbus, Ohio: Merrill.

SALTZMAN, HENRY, 1963, "The Community School in an Urban Setting," in *Education in Depressed Areas,* A. Harry Passow, ed. New York: Teachers College Press, Columbia University.

SAVA, SAMUEL G., 1968, "When Learning Comes Easy," *Saturday Review,* November 16, pp. 102 ff.

SCHREIBER, WILLIAM I., 1962, *Our Amish Neighbors.* Chicago: University of Chicago Press.

SIMONS, MENNO, 1956, *The Complete Writings of Menno Simons.* Scottdale, Pa.: Herald Press.

SIZER, THEODORE, 1969, "The Case for a Free Market," *Saturday Review,* January 11, pp. 34 ff.

SPINDLER, GEORGE D., 1963, *Education and Culture—Anthropological Approaches.* New York: Holt, Rinehart and Winston, Inc.

STOLL, JOSEPH, 1963, *The Challenge of the Child.* Aylmer, Ontario: Pathway Publishing Corporation (Second edition, 1967).

———, 1965, *Who Shall Educate Our Children?* Aylmer, Ontario: Pathway Publishing Corporation.

STOLTZFUS, GRANT M., 1954, *History of the First Amish Mennonite Communities in America.* M.A. thesis. University of Pittsburgh.

WAX, MURRAY, ROSALIE WAX, AND ROBERT DUMONT, 1964, *Education in an American Indian Community.* Social Problems Monograph. Atlanta: Emory University.

WELLS, RICHARD D., 1967, *Articles of Agreement Regarding the Indiana Amish Parochial Schools and Department of Public Instruction.* Indianapolis, Ind.: Department of Public Instruction, Richard D. Wells, Superintendent.

WITTMER, JOE, 1970, "Homogeneity of Personality Characteristics: A Comparison between Old Order Amish and Non-Amish," *American Anthropologist* 72:1063–1068.

YOUNG, MICHAEL, AND PATRICK MCGEENEY, 1968, *Learning Begins at Home: A Study of a Junior School and Its Parents.* London: Routledge. Institute of Community Studies.

ZOOK, NOAH, 1963, *Seeking a Better Country.* Gordonville, Pa.: Old Order Book Society.